The Catholic Charismatic Renewal, Revisited

FATHER RAY INTROVIGNE, M. DIV.
WILLIAM AYLES, D.D.

EN ROUTE BOOKS AND MEDIA, LLC
SAINT LOUIS, MO

Make the time

En Route Books and Media, LLC
5705 Rhodes Avenue
St. Louis, MO 63109

Contact us at contactus@enroutebooksandmedia.com

Cover art: The symbolic fresco of Jesus knocking on your door in Herz Jesu Church in Vienna, Austria, from the beginning of the 20th Century. Licensed with Alamy.

Copyright 2025 Ray Introvigne and William Ayles

ISBN: 979-8-88870-316-8
Library of Congress Control Number:
Available online at https://catalog.loc.gov

The Scriptures in this book are taken from the New Revised Standard Version, Catholic Edition. The papal documents included in Chapter 2 © Dicastero per la Comunicazione-Libreria Editrice Vaticana; used with permission.

All rights reserved. No part of this book may be reproduced, stored in a retrieval system, or transmitted in any form, or by any means, electronic, mechanical, photocopying, or otherwise, without the prior written permission of the author.

Table of Contents

Co-Author's Note iii

Act One 1
    1. YOUR RENEWAL 3
    2. The Holy Fathers 15
    3. My Testimony 45

Act Two 77
    4. Our Lord 79
    5. Peter 89
    6. Luke 95
    7. Paul 101
    8. James 107
    9. Jude 109

Addenda 111

Acknowledgments 113

Co-Author's Note

The Catholic Charismatic Renewal affected me in a profound manner: I received the Baptism of the Holy Spirit to overflowing—and spoke forth the divine sign known as speaking in "new tongues" (the language of the Holy Spirit).

> It transformed my life and my ministry.
> Truly, I received the Holy Spirit EXPERIENCE.
> Christ's love, joy, and peace flooded my soul.

This Holy Spirit Renewal awakened me: The power of the Holy Spirit produced a "head-to-heart experience"—which continues to mean so much to me.

I was never the same and I have never looked back. I thank God for this wonderful blessing.

My hope is that you may have the same Holy Spirit EXPERIENCE—and know what it means to "fall in love with our Lord and Savior, Jesus Christ." Your life will be renewed from that moment forward. And just like the disciples on Pentecost, you will be ushered into the language of the Church: speaking in the Holy Spirit language, "new tongues." Christ Himself proclaimed this for us! Please know it is an unexpected conversion experience.

Truly, I want this book to be a beacon of divine light for you.

In this book, you will hear from many voices. You will hear from students who experienced the Holy Spirit Renewal; you will hear from our Holy Fathers: St. Pope John XXIII, St. Pope Paul VI, St. Pope John Paul II, Pope Benedict XVI, and Pope

Francis; you will hear from our first-century disciples, and from Christ Himself. Additionally, you'll hear my testimony—which I hope will speak to you.

Finally, this is my prayer for you:

"Our Father in Heaven, I ask that You intervene in the lives of those reading this book, those who are searching. Let the Holy Spirit Renewal—the 'New Pentecost'—become real. Dear Father, as Your Son said, let 'rivers of living water'—the Holy Spirit—overflow from their hearts, immersing them in Your love, joy, and peace—like they've never known before. I pray this in the precious name of Your Son, Jesus."

God Bless each of you in an "Extra Special Way."

—Father Ray Introvigne

Act One

1
YOUR RENEWAL

> "Renew Your wonders in this our day,
> as by a new Pentecost."
>
> —St. Pope John XXIII, 1962,
> Vatican II Prayer

Five years after St. Pope John XXIII prayed for a "NEW PENTECOST," our Lord responded. This belief is universally accepted by our modern-day Holy Fathers.

Our Lord—through the Holy Spirit—ignited the Catholic Charismatic Renewal, bringing forth our NEW PENTECOST! This work of the Holy Spirit is a blessing and an extension of Vatican II. With this Renewal, the work of the Holy Spirit began afresh.

In 1967, Catholics began to EXPERIENCE what the disciples experienced nearly 2000 years earlier. And to recognize this work of the Holy Spirit, Pope Francis hosted the 50th anniversary of the Catholic Charismatic Renewal: The Golden Jubilee Celebration in 2017. This celebration recognized the NEW PENTECOST that St. Pope John XXIII prayed for—which St. Pope Paul VI subsequently called, "a chance for the Church and the world," and Pope Francis called a "flood of grace" in the Church.

At the Golden Jubilee, Pope Francis stood on stage with Patti Mansfield, one of the first Catholics to EXPERIENCE the Baptism of the Holy Spirit—which overflowed with divine power. She witnessed the very start of the Catholic Charismatic Renewal.

It all started in February 1967 at The Ark and the Dove

retreat house...

Dozens of Duquesne University students attended a spiritual retreat and EXPERIENCED "divine intervention": the Baptism of the Holy Spirit overflowed into the gift of the Holy Spirit language. This is the same gift our Lord had prophesied on the day of His Ascension: It is the divine sign of the Holy Spirit language, known as "new tongues" (Mark 16:17).

This sign of "new tongues" graced those at the retreat: One by one, the Holy Spirit showered the students with this gift!

Prior to the retreat, the students were instructed to "pray with expectant faith." And they were asked to read the first four chapters of the Acts of the Apostles (also known as the Book of Acts.)

Unbeknownst to all, this retreat would mark a new day for the Roman Catholic Church and the world: It heralded the starting point of the Catholic Charismatic Renewal. The windows of Heaven opened, and our Lord poured out His blessing in a wonderful way: a NEW PENTECOST! Praise God!

You—as a follower of Christ—deserve to understand this blessing.

You—as a follower of Christ—deserve to receive this "Holy Spirit EXPERIENCE."

Now, let's go back to this magnificent moment in time: the blessed events at The Ark and the Dove retreat house. You will hear from two of the original Duquesne students: David Mangan and Patti Mansfield. Each received the Holy Spirit EXPERIENCE of Renewal. God's divine power poured forth: *They spoke in languages of the Holy Spirit—while being immersed in God's love, joy, and peace.* You will also hear from a Catholic teacher, Dorothy Ranaghan, who witnessed the change in these students.

Dorothy, David, and Patti's testimonies are taken from highly informative videos (noted at the chapter's end).

Chapter One: Your Renewal

Finally, you will hear from Monsignor Vincent M. Walsh, who describes how the Renewal spread quickly from that first outpouring.

Let's begin with David and Patti's testimonies from the video, "Exploring the Roots of the Catholic Charismatic Renewal."

David Mangan's Experience

Narrator: "One of the speakers taught from Jesus' words in [the Book of] Acts 1:8: 'But you will receive power when the Holy Spirit comes upon you.'"

David: "The word for 'power' is the same Greek word where we in English would get the word 'dynamite.' And he [the retreat speaker] likened the coming of the Holy Spirit to dynamite. And that struck me extremely deeply because although I'd been raised a good Catholic boy, and I was with the Lord, and he hadn't abandoned me at all, and I knew that's where I belonged, and where I was, but I don't think I could have used the word 'dynamite' as an adjective to describe my spiritual life at that point."

Narrator: "David joined his small group session and asked a question, 'Where is the dynamite?' He later recorded in his notes his desire to hear someone speak in tongues."

David: "Then I put a dash, and I put 'me' [to speak in tongues] with an exclamation point!"

Narrator: "David went off by himself to reflect on the teaching."

David: "When I opened the door and walked into the chapel, the presence of God was so powerful I could hardly move. The only way I could say is, 'I was lost in Christ, and happy to be so.' And I completely forgot about all my pushing to say, 'where's the dynamite?' 'where's the dynamite?' That's exactly what it felt like. It felt like little explosions in my body were going off as part of this whole experience. I don't even know how to describe it beyond that. I start opening my mouth to thank God for what he had done, and I start praying in another language.... Everything changed at that point. Now, I didn't spot it all right away, but I mean everything was different, as it turned out, after this happened to me."

Patti Mansfield's Experience

Narrator: "Later, Patti joined David in the chapel."

Patti: "I began to tremble. I remember thinking God is here. And He's holy, and I'm not holy. And so just kneeling there in the quiet of my heart, I said, 'Father, I give my life to you. Whatever you ask, I accept it.' I was lying there prostrate, and I felt immersed in the love of God. I felt like I was swimming in the mercy of God. I remember thinking, just saying to Him, 'stay, stay, stay.'"

Narrator: "Other students were also drawn into the chapel."

Patti: "Some people were *laughing for joy*; others were *weeping for joy*. Some said they felt like they wanted to praise God, but they didn't know if it was going to come out in English. Anyway, we were there, and just in awe—*just in awe*—of the sovereign God."

Narrator: "The small gathering of Duquesne students who walked away from that retreat center say they were never the same, but what they didn't know at the time was that their life-changing experience was meant to be shared. And it was just the beginning."

Dorothy Ranaghan's Experience

Dorothy Ranaghan's testimony comes from the video, "Fifty Years of the Catholic Charismatic Movement: 1967-2017."

Dorothy: "We could see that even in their faces there was something changed… and different.… [W]e could not deny the EXPERIENCE we saw they had… [it] had changed them. And whatever it was, I think we came to see we wanted that, too. *We wanted more.*"

David Mangan's Interview

David gives us a detailed account of his Holy Spirit EXPERIENCE at The Ark and the Dove retreat house. David was the first student in the chapel to experience this Renewal. His testimony is found in the video, "Forerunners: E06 - David Mangan."

When the narrator asked David about how the Holy Spirit EXPERIENCE spread to other students, David said something profound: *"The Holy Spirit was working on people with open hearts."*

And during the interview, David also spoke of the book he authored: *GOD LOVES YOU and there is nothing you can do about it.*

Monsignor Vincent M. Walsh

In his book, *What is Going On,* Monsignor Walsh wrote about how the Renewal caught fire within the Catholic community:

"The news of the [Catholic Charismatic Renewal] movement spread to students at Notre Dame through a visitor from Duquesne. Two other important personalities, Ralph Martin and Steve Clark, who were working at Michigan State, visited Duquesne to receive their own Baptism of the Spirit.

"On April 7, 1967, groups from these two universities gathered at Notre Dame. Their meeting attracted national attention through two widely read Catholic newspapers, *The National Catholic Reporter* (April 19, 1967) and *Our Sunday Visitor* (May 14, 1967). With these reports, Catholics realized, for the first time, that people in the 20th century could pray in tongues."[1]

Why Pray in Tongues?

The apostle Paul told us,

"Likewise the Spirit helps us in our weakness; for we do not know how to pray as we ought, but that very Spirit intercedes with sighs too deep for words. And God, who searches the heart, knows what is the mind of the Spirit, because the Spirit intercedes for the saints according to the will of God. We know that all things work together for good for those who love God, who are called according to his purpose" (Rom. 8:26–28).

When we pray in the Holy Spirit language, the Spirit intercedes for us. Let us therefore call upon the power of the Holy Spirit—by praying in the Spirit. This is precisely what Jude asked of us. He said, "beloved, build yourselves up on your most holy faith; pray in the Holy Spirit" (Jude 20).

Brothers and sisters in Christ: If it is the will of our God that we pray in the language of the Holy Spirit, then let us respond with humility. Let us respond with our holy zeal. That is exactly what the apostle Paul asked of us: "Pursue love and strive for the spiritual gifts" (1 Cor. 14:1). Your Holy Spirit EXPERIENCE awaits!

Your Renewal: Faith and Humility

Yes, God loves you and there *is* nothing you can do about it.
Let your heart be open to Him.
Faith and humility set the stage for YOUR Holy Spirit EXPERIENCE.

Faith

Faith comes from hearing the words of Christ.
Faith is the fire that kindles your Renewal.
Now, listen to what Paul said to us regarding the message of faith:

"([T]he word of faith that we proclaim); because if you confess with your lips that Jesus is Lord and believe in your heart that God raised him from the dead, you will be saved. For one believes with the heart and so is justified, and one confesses with the mouth and so is saved. The scripture says, 'No one who believes in him will be put to shame.'... For, 'Everyone who calls on the name of the Lord shall be saved.'... So faith comes from what is heard, and what is heard comes through the word of Christ" (Rom. 10:8–11, 13, 17).

Hallelujah!! We have received the message of faith—the Good News!!

Now...
Declare Jesus, the Son of God, to be *your* Lord!
Declare the miracle of the Resurrection!
By declaring Him as Lord, we embrace His sacrifice on the Cross.
We declare... He died as the perfect sacrifice for sin.
We declare... He took upon Himself sin and the wages of sin—which is death.
We declare... He died in our place, saving us.
We declare... His sacrificial blood cleanses our sins.
We declare... we embrace His message of faith.

Your Holy Spirit EXPERIENCE begins with faith.
And your Holy Spirit EXPERIENCE begins with humility.

Humility

Consider what our dear Lord said to the little children (who have humble hearts): "Let the little children come to me, and do not stop them; for it is to such as these that the kingdom of heaven belongs" (Matt. 19:14).

Allow your humble heart (as little children) to be open to the work of the Holy Spirit because with "God, all things are possible" (Matt. 19:26).

Catholic Charismatic Renewal Today

Today, it is estimated that there are over 300 million Charismatic Catholics. The word "Charismatic" is derived from the Greek word *Charismata* which comes from the Greek word *Charis,* meaning "grace" or "favor." *Charismata* is the plural form of the Greek word *Charisma* which means a "gift of grace."[2] Charismatic Catholics have chosen to embrace this grace and favor of our Lord.

Our Lord bestows upon us His grace and favor—which takes the form of spiritual gifts. And the apostle Paul implored us to be zealous for spiritual gifts and matters. And Paul reassured us that these spiritual gifts shall remain active in Christ's Church until the Second Advent: the revealing of our Lord and Savior. Paul told us: "you are not lacking in any spiritual gift [*Charisma*] as you wait for the revealing of our Lord Jesus Christ" (1 Cor. 1:7). The will of the Holy Spirit is that Christ's Church lacks nothing regarding spiritual gifts—as we wait for the return of our Lord.

Until that day, we seek His grace and favor; we seek His guidance; we seek out those in the Church who stand ready to assist in our spiritual quest for this spiritual gift of new tongues.

Catholic Charismatic Renewal Resources

In our day and time, several resources are available to you—including these:

- Renewal Ministries: www.renewalministries.net. (734) 662-1730. Renewal Ministries offers the "Life in the

Spirit" video "As by a New Pentecost: Seven Teachings to Prepare for a New Life in the Spirit." It's available via CD or MP3 at Renewal Ministries' website. It's also available on their YouTube channel (search "As by a New Pentecost" at www.youtube.com/renewalministries). "Renewal Ministries seeks to foster renewal in the Catholic Church through the power of the Holy Spirit for the salvation of souls." They also offer additional Catholic Charismatic Renewal resources at www.renewalministries.net/catholic-charismatic-renewal-resources.

- The Ark and the Dove Retreat House: https://www.thearkandthedoveworldwide.org/en/
- "A.C.T.S." (Adoration, Community, Theology, Service) Seminar/ Retreat. Patricia LaPointe, 19 Oakland Ter., Manchester, CT 06042.
- "Awakening to the Holy Spirit" Seminar/Retreat. Mrs. Andrea Hoisl, Director of Faith Events, 331 Main Street, Norwich, CT 06360.

This book, *The Catholic Charismatic Renewal, Revisited*, is all about our awesome Holy Spirit who offers each of us as brothers and sisters a PACKAGED PENTECOST EXPERIENCE.

Why not order the "Life in the Spirit" video? (734) 662-1730. Why not pray for Jesus to bless and Baptize you in the Holy Spirit with power?

We thank God that the Catholic Charismatic Renewal testifies to the work of the Holy Spirit in our day and time. And this is what the Catholic Charismatic Renewal is all about: *Your Personal Renewal!*

Catholic Charismatic Renewal Videos

YOUTUBE QR CODES*

1. Exploring the Roots of the Catholic Charismatic Renewal

2. Fifty Years of the Catholic Charismatic Movement: 1967-2017

3. Forerunners: E06 - David Mangan

1. Monsignor Vincent M. Walsh, *What is Going On* (Wynnewood, PA: Key of David Publications, 1995), pp. 86, 87.

2. E. W. Bullinger, *A Critical Lexicon and Concordance to the English and Greek New Testament* (Grand Rapids, MI: Zondervan Publishing House, 1995), p. 318.

*Scanning the QR code will open the YouTube webpage link to the video. We invite you to watch these priceless testimonies. To scan the QR code, use your phone's camera (as if you were going to take a photo). Center the QR code on the screen. You will need to hold it for a few seconds, and a link will appear on the screen (at the top, or bottom, or right below the QR code). Tap the link to open the webpage/video.

2
The Holy Fathers

"So that she can fulfill her mission, the Holy Spirit 'bestows upon [the Church] varied hierarchic and charismatic gifts, and in this way directs her.'"

—Catechism of the Catholic Church, p. 768

All of our Holy Fathers, beginning with St. Pope John XXIII, have embraced the transforming, renewing power of the Holy Spirit: a NEW PENTECOST. Each pope has taken the time to actively encourage all Roman Catholics to follow their lead—and to follow the lead of our Lord and His apostles.

What follows are the words of our Holy Fathers.

We begin with St. Pope John XXIII. He had the foresight to call for a new day in the Church: Vatican II. He knew the time had arrived to open the stained-glass windows to a Holy Spirit Renewal.

From Vatican II, the Catholic Charismatic Renewal would spring!

St. Pope John XXIII

"**St. Pope John XXIII** prayed in 1962 for 'a new Pentecost.' In preparation for the Second Vatican Council, he prayed for God to,

> 'Renew Your wonders in this our day, as by a new Pentecost. Grant to Your Church that, being of one mind and steadfast in prayer with Mary, the Mother of Jesus, and

following the lead of blessed Peter, it may advance the reign of our Divine Savior, the reign of truth and justice, the reign of love and peace. Amen.'"[1]

Note: St. Pope John XXIII died in June 1963. St. Pope Paul VI was unanimously elected and carried out St. Pope John XXIII's Holy Spirit guidance perfectly.

St. Pope Paul VI

"In May 1975, **Pope Paul VI** welcomed 10,000 Catholic charismatics who were attending an International Conference on the Charismatic Renewal in the Church in Rome. In his address to them, Pope Paul stated,

Chapter Two: The Holy Fathers

> 'As we said last October in the presence of some of you, the Church and the world need more than ever that "miracle of Pentecost should continue in history".... Nothing is more necessary to this increasingly secularized world than the witness of this "spiritual renewal" that we see the Holy Spirit evoking in the most diverse regions and milieu. How then could this spiritual renewal not be good fortune (sometimes translated "a chance") for the church and for the world?'"[2]

"After completing his prepared message, Pope Paul gave a spontaneous word of support.

> 'Have we forgotten the Holy Spirit? Certainly not! We want him, we honor him, and we love him. And you with your devotion, your fervor, your wish to live in the Spirit: this should be. It ought to rejuvenate the world, give it back a spirituality, a soul, a religious thought; it ought to reopen the world's closed lips to prayer and open its mouth to song, to joy, to hymns, and to witnessing. It will be very fortunate for our time and for our brothers that there should be a whole generation – your generation of young people – who shout out to the world the glory and greatness of the God of Pentecost.'"[3]

Note: St. Pope Paul VI died in 1978.

St. Pope John Paul II

"In December 1979, **St. Pope John Paul II** in a private audience with the ICCRO Council [International Catholic Charismatic Renewal Offices] said,

Chapter Two: The Holy Fathers

'I am convinced that this movement is a sign of His action (of the Spirit). The world is much in need of this action of the Holy Spirit, and it needs many instruments for this action. Now I see this movement, this activity everywhere.'"[4]

"To the Italian National Service Committee in April 1998 [St. Pope John Paul II said] -

'The Catholic charismatic movement is one of the many fruits of the Second Vatican Council, which, like a new Pentecost, led to an extraordinary flourishing in the Church's life of groups and movements particularly sensitive to the action of the Spirit. How can we not give *thanks* for the *precious spiritual fruits* that the Renewal has produced in the life of the Church and in the lives of so many people? How many lay faithful – men, women, young people, adults and elderly – have been able to experience in their own lives the amazing power of the Spirit and his gifts! How many people have rediscovered faith, the joy of prayer, the power and beauty of the Word of God, translating all this into generous service in the Church's mission! How many lives have been profoundly changed! For all this today, together with you, I wish to praise and thank the Holy Spirit.'"[5]

THE CHURCH WISHES TO SPREAD CHRIST'S FIRE IN HUMAN HEARTS

St. POPE JOHN PAUL II's PENTECOST EVE ADDRESS MAY 1998

"In Jerusalem, almost 2000 years ago, on the day of Pentecost, before an astonished and mocking crowd, due to the unexplainable change observed in the Apostles, Peter courageously proclaims: 'Jesus of Nazareth, a man attested to you by God... you crucified and killed by the hands of lawless men. But God raised him up' (Acts 2:22-24). Peter's words express the Church's self-awareness, based on the certainty that Jesus Christ is alive, [and] are working in the present and changes life.

"The Holy Spirit, already at work in the creation of the world and in the Old Covenant, reveals himself in the Incarnation and Paschal Mystery of the Son of God, and in a way 'bursts out' at Pentecost to extend the mission of Christ the Lord in time and space. The Spirit thus makes the church a stream of new life that flows through the history of mankind.

"With the Second Vatican Council, the Comforter recently gave the Church, which according to the Fathers in the place 'where the Spirit flourishes' (Catechism of the Catholic Church, n. 749) a renewed Pentecost, instilling a new and unforeseen dynamism.

"Whenever the Spirit intervenes, He leaves people astonished. He brings about events of amazing newness; He radically changes persons and history. This was the unforgettable experience of the Second Vatican Ecumenical Council during which, under the guidance of the same

Spirit, the Church rediscovered the charismatic dimension as one of her constitutive [essential] elements.

"It is not only through the sacraments and the ministrations of the Church that the Holy Spirit makes holy the people, leads them and enriches them with his virtues. Allotting His gifts according as He wills (cf. 1 Cor. 12:11), He also distributes special graces among the faithful of every rank... He makes them fit and ready to undertake various tasks and offices for the renewal and building up of the Church (*Lumen Gentium*, n. 12).

"You are tangible proof of the Spirit's outpouring....

"Today, I would like to cry out to all of you gathered here in Saint Peter's Square and to all Christians: ***Open yourselves docilely [submissively] to the gifts of the Spirit. Accept gratefully and obediently the charisms which the Spirit never ceases to bestow on us! Do not forget that every charism is given for the common good, that is, for the benefits of the whole Church.***

"By their nature, charisms are communicative and give rise to that 'spiritual affinity between persons' (*Christifideles laici*, n. 24) and that friendship in Christ which is the origin of 'movements.'...

"Jesus said, 'I came and cast fire upon the earth; and would that it were already kindled!' (Luke 12:39). As the Church prepares to cross the threshold of the third millennium, let us accept the Lord's invitation, so that His fire may spread in our hearts and in those of our brothers and sisters.

"Today, from this upper room in St. Peter's Square, a great prayer rises: 'Come Holy Spirit,' come and renew the face of the earth! Come with your seven gifts! Come, Spirit of Life, Spirit of Communion and Love! The Church and the world need you.

"Come, Holy Spirit, and make ever more fruitful the charisms you have bestowed on us. Give new strength and missionary zeal to these sons and of daughters of yours who have gathered here. Open their hearts; renew their Christian commitment in the world. Make them courageous messengers of the Gospel, witnesses to the risen Jesus Christ, the Redeemer and Savior of man. Strengthen their love and their fidelity to the Church....

"Today, from this square, Christ says to each of you: 'Go into all the world and preach the gospel to the whole creation' (Mk 16:15). He is counting on every one of you, and so is the Church. 'Lo,' the Lord promises, 'I am with you always to the close of the age' (Mt 28:20). [I] ... am with you. Amen.

"[I] ... pray that the Holy Spirit will increase the flame of His love in your hearts so that you may be ever more effective in bringing the Gospel message to the world of the new millennium. The Church needs your commitment and your love!"[6]

Pope Emeritus Benedict XVI

"Address of **Pope Emeritus Benedict XVI** to Charismatic Covenant Communities October 2008 -

'What we learn in the New Testament on charisms, which appeared as visible signs of the coming of the Holy Spirit, *is not a historical event of the past, but a reality ever alive.* It is the same divine Spirit, soul of the Church, that acts in every age and those mysterious and effective interventions of the Spirit are manifest in our time in a providential way. The Movements and New Communities are like an outpouring of the Holy Spirit in the Church and in contemporary society. We can, therefore, rightly say that one of the positive elements and aspects of the Community of the Catholic Charismatic Renewal is precisely their emphasis on the charisms or gifts of the Holy Spirit and their merit lies in having recalled their topicality [relevance] in the Church.'"[7]

"May 26, 2012 address to participants in the meeting sponsored by 'Renewal in the Holy Spirit' -

'Dear friends of Renewal in the Holy Spirit, do not grow weary of turning to Heaven: the world stands in need of prayer. It needs men and women who feel the attraction of Heaven in their life, who make praise to the Lord a new way of life. And may you be joyful Christians! I entrust you all to Mary Most Holy, present in the Upper Room at the event of Pentecost. Persevere with her in prayer, walk guided by the light of the living Holy Spirit, proclaiming the Good News of Christ.'"[8]

Pope Francis

All the popes—since St. Pope John XXIII—have actively supported the Holy Spirit Renewal: the NEW PENTECOST in the Church.

Yet, why is it many followers of Christ in the Roman Catholic Church have never heard of—nor have taken an interest in—the Renewal?

On April 17, 2013, Pope Francis addressed root causes of this issue. The Holy Father said that rejecting the Holy Spirit's work in Vatican II is "foolish."

From Vatican City, Pope Francis spoke, and the Catholic News Agency (CNA) gave us this news account.

REJECTING HOLY SPIRIT'S WORK IN VATICAN II IS "FOOLISH," POPE SAYS

ADDRESS OF HIS HOLINESS POPE FRANCIS

"'The work of the Holy Spirit at the Second Vatican Council is not yet finished,' Pope Francis said, 'because many in the Church are unwilling to fully embrace what God inspired in the council fathers.'

"In his homily at an April 16 Mass at St. Martha's Residence, the Pope observed that the Holy Spirit always 'moves us, makes us walk and pushes the Church forward.'

"However, he said, we often respond by saying, 'Don't bother us.'

"'We want to put the Holy Spirit to sleep,' the Pontiff noted. 'We want to "tame" the Holy Spirit. And that doesn't work, because He is God. He is the wind that comes and goes and we know not from where.

"'He is the strength of God, the one who gives us comfort and drives us to continue forward,' Pope Francis continued.

Chapter Two: The Holy Fathers

But the idea of 'going forward' is what often bothers us, because we want to 'remain comfortable,' he explained.

"'This temptation is still here today,' the Holy Father observed, pointing [to] the Second Vatican Council as an example.

"'The Council was a beautiful work of the Holy Spirit,' he stressed.

"'But after 50 years have we done everything that the Holy Spirit told us at the Council?' he asked, questioning whether the Church currently contains the council's 'continuity of growth.'

"'No,' he answered.

"Some Catholics want to 'build a monument' to the council without being willing to change, the Pope lamented. 'And what's more, there are some who want to turn back. This is called being stubborn, this is called wanting to tame the Holy Spirit, this called being foolish and slow of heart,' he stressed.

"The same thing happens with our own personal lives, the Holy Father continued, explaining that we often resist when 'the Holy Spirit pushes us to take a more evangelical path. Do not resist the Holy Spirit,' Pope Francis urged. 'It is the Spirit that makes us free, with that freedom of Jesus, that freedom of the children of God!

"'This is the grace that I wish all of us would ask of the Lord: docility [submission] to the Holy Spirit, to that Spirit who comes to us and makes us advance down the path of holiness, that holiness of the Church that is so beautiful,' the Pope concluded."[9]

THE HOLY SPIRIT CANNOT BE CAGED

Pope Francis addressed the Catholic Charismatic Renewal at the 37th National Convocation of the Renewal of the Holy Spirit in Rome on June 1, 2014.

ADDRESS OF HIS HOLINESS POPE FRANCIS

"Thank you so much for your welcome. Someone must have told today's organizers that I really like the hymn: 'Jesus the Lord lives.' When I would celebrate Mass in the cathedral at Buenos Aires with the charismatic renewal, after the consecration and a few moments of adoration in tongues, we would sing this hymn with great joy and fervor, as you have today. Thank you! I felt at home!

"I thank Renewal in the Spirit, ICCRS and the Catholic Fraternity for this opportunity to be with you, which is a source of great joy for me. I am grateful for the presence here of the first members of the renewal, who had an intense experience of the Holy Spirit's power. I believe that Patti [Mansfield] is here... You, the charismatic renewal, have received a great gift from the Lord. Your movement's birth was willed by the Holy Spirit to be 'a current of grace in the Church and for the Church.' This is your identity: to be a current of grace.

"What was the very first gift of the Holy Spirit? It is the gift of himself, the one who is love and who makes us fall in love with Jesus. And this love changes our lives. That is why we speak of 'being born again in the Spirit.' It is what Jesus told Nicodemus. You have received the great gift of diversity of charisms, the diversity which becomes harmony in the Holy Spirit, and in service to the Church.

Chapter Two: The Holy Fathers

"When I think of charismatics, I think of the Church herself, but in a particular way: I think of a great orchestra, where all the instruments and voices are different from one another, yet all are needed to create the harmony of the music. Saint Paul speaks of this in the twelfth chapter of the First Letter to the Corinthians. As in an orchestra, no one in the renewal can think of himself or herself as being more important or greater than the others, please! Because when you think of yourselves as more important or greater, disaster is already on the horizon! No one can say: 'I am the head.' Like the Church, you have only one head, one Lord, the Lord Jesus.

"Repeat with me: Who is the head of the renewal? The Lord Jesus!

"Who is head of the renewal?"

[The crowd:] "The Lord Jesus!"

"And we can say this with the power given us by the Holy Spirit, since no one can say 'Jesus is Lord' without the Holy Spirit.

"As you may know—because the news gets around—in the first years of the charismatic renewal in Buenos Aires, I didn't care very much for charismatics. I used to think: 'They strike me as some kind of samba school!' I didn't share their style of prayer or the many new things which were happening in the Church. Later, I got to know them and I finally realized all the good that the charismatic renewal was doing for the Church. And this story which began with the 'samba school' had an unexpected ending: a few months before entering the conclave, I was named the spiritual assistant for the charismatic renewal in Argentina by the Conference of Bishops.

"The charismatic renewal is a great force meant to serve the preaching of the Gospel in the joy of the Holy Spirit. You received the Holy Spirit and he has made you appreciate God's love for all his children; he has also made you love God's word. In the early days, they used to say that you charismatics always carried around a Bible, the New Testament... Do you still carry one today?"

[The crowd:] "Yes!"

"I'm not so sure! If not, return to this first love, and always carry the Word of God in your pocket or bag! And read a bit of it. Keep the word of God with you always."

"You, the people of God, the people of the charismatic renewal, must be careful not to lose the freedom which the Holy Spirit has given you! The danger for the renewal, as our dear Father Raniero Cantalamessa often says, is that of getting too organized: the danger of excessive planning.

"Yes, you need organization, but never lose the grace of letting God be God! 'Yet there is no greater freedom than that of allowing oneself to be guided by the Holy Spirit, renouncing the attempt to plan and control everything to the last detail, and instead letting him enlighten, guide, and direct us, leading us wherever he wills. The Holy Spirit knows well what is needed in every time and place. This is what it means to be mysteriously fruitful!'" (*Evangelii Gaudium, 280*).

Chapter Two: The Holy Fathers

"Another danger is that of becoming arbiters of God's grace. Many times, leaders (I prefer the name 'servants') of a group or community become, perhaps without intending to, 'managers' of grace, deciding who can receive the prayer of outpouring or baptism in the Spirit and who cannot. If any of you are doing this, I ask you to stop; no more! You are dispensers of God's grace, not its arbiters. Don't act like a tollhouse for the Holy Spirit!

"In the *Malines Documents*, you have a guide, a reliable path to keep you from going astray. The first document is *Theological and Pastoral Orientations*. The second is *Ecumenism and Charismatic Renewal*, written by Cardinal Suenens himself, an outstanding figure of the Second Vatican Council. The third is *Charismatic Renewal and Social Action*, written by Cardinal Suenens and Bishop Helder Camara.

"This is your path: evangelization, spiritual ecumenism, caring for the poor and needy, and welcoming the marginalized. And all of it is based on worship! The foundation of the renewal is worshiping God!

"They asked me to tell you what the Pope expects of you.

"The first thing is conversion to the love of Jesus which changes our lives and makes each Christian a witness to God's love. The Church expects this witness of Christian life from us, and the Holy Spirit helps us to live the Gospel fully and consistently for our own growth and holiness.

"I expect you to share with everyone in the Church the grace of baptism in the Holy Spirit (a phrase we find in the Acts of the Apostles).

"I expect you to evangelize with the Word of God, which proclaims that Jesus lives and that he loves all men and women.

"To give a witness of spiritual ecumenism to all our brothers and sisters of other Churches and Christian communities who believe in Jesus as Lord and Savior.

"To remain united in the love that the Lord Jesus asks us to have for all people, and in prayer to the Holy Spirit for the attainment of this unity which is necessary for evangelization in the name of Jesus. Remember that 'the charismatic renewal is de facto ecumenical in nature ... The Catholic renewal rejoices in what the Holy Spirit is accomplishing in the other Churches' (*1 Malines 5, 3*).

"Be close to the poor and to those in need, so as to touch in their flesh the wounded flesh of Jesus. Please, draw near to them!

"Seek unity in their renewal, because unity comes from the Holy Spirit and is born of the unity of the Trinity. Who is the source of division? The devil! Division comes from the devil. Flee from all infighting, please! Let there be none of this among you!

"I wish to thank ICCRS and Catholic Fraternity, the two groups of pontifical right and of Pontifical Council for the Laity which are at the service of the worldwide renewal and are entrusted with preparing the world meeting of priests and Bishops in June of next year. I know that they have decided to work together and to share office space as a sign of unity and to make better use of their resources. This makes me very happy. I would also like to thank them because they are already working on preparations for the great jubilee of 2017.

"Brothers and sisters remember: Worship the Lord your God. This is fundamental! Worship God. Seek holiness in the new life of the Holy Spirit. Be dispensers of the grace of God. Avoid the danger of excessive organization.

"Go out into the streets and evangelize. Proclaim the Gospel. Remember that the church was born 'on the move,' that Pentecost morning. Draw close to the poor and touch in their flesh the wounded flesh of Jesus. Let yourselves be guided by the Holy Spirit, in freedom; and please, don't put the Holy Spirit in a cage!

"Be free!

"Seek unity in the renewal, the unity which comes from the Trinity!

"And I am waiting for all of you, charismatics the world over, to participate with the Pope you're a great jubilee on the feast of Pentecost 2017 in Saint Peter's square! Thank you!"[10]

POPE FRANCIS' PENTECOST EVE ADDRESS, JUNE 2017

In June 2017, **Pope Francis** hosted the 50th anniversary—the Golden Jubilee—celebration of the Catholic Charismatic Renewal. Over 50,000 attendees from over 120 countries attended this celebration. What follows is his opening address.

PENTECOST VIGIL OF PRAYER
ADDRESS OF HIS HOLINESS POPE FRANCIS
Circus Maximus
Saturday, 3 June 2017

"Brothers and sisters, thank you for the witness you have given here today, thank you! It has helped us all, myself included... all of us!

"In the first chapter of the Acts of the Apostles we read: 'And staying with them, [Jesus] charged them not to depart from Jerusalem, but to wait for the promise of the Father, about which, he said, "you heard from me, for John baptized with water, but before many days, you will be baptized with the Holy Spirit"' (*Acts* 1:4-5).

"'When the day of Pentecost had come, they were all together in one place. And suddenly a sound came from heaven like the rush of a mighty wind, and it filled the house where they were sitting. And there appeared to them tongues as of fire, distributed and resting on each of them. And they were all filled with the Holy Spirit and began to speak in other tongues, as the Spirit gave them utterance' (*Acts* 2:1-4).

"Today we are here in a kind of Upper Room beneath the open sky, unafraid, under the open sky and with our hearts open to the promise of the Father. 'All of us who believe' have gathered here, all of us who confess that 'Jesus is Lord.' Many have come from different parts of the world, and the Holy Spirit has brought us together to build bonds of fraternal friendship that encourage us on our journey towards unity, unity for mission. Not to stand still! But for mission, to proclaim that Jesus is Lord – *Jesús es el Señor*.

"To proclaim together the love of the Father for all his children. To proclaim the Good News to all peoples. To demonstrate that peace is possible. It is not so easy to show this world today that peace is possible, but in the name of Jesus we can show by our testimony that peace is possible! It is possible if we are at peace with one another. If we emphasize our differences, we are at war among ourselves and we cannot proclaim peace. Peace is possible, based on our confession that Jesus is Lord and on our evangelization along this path. It is possible. Even by showing that we have differences – this is obvious, we have differences – but that we desire to be a *reconciled diversity*. We should not forget that phrase, but say it to everyone: reconciled diversity. The phrase is not mine. It comes from a Lutheran brother. Reconciled diversity.

"Now we are here and we are many! We have gathered to pray together, to ask the Holy Spirit to come upon each of us, so that we can go forth into the streets of the city and the world to proclaim the lordship of Jesus Christ.

"In the Book of Acts we read: 'Parthians and Medes and Elamites and residents of Mesopotamia, Judea and Cappadocia, Pontus and Asia, Phrygia and Pamphylia, Egypt and the parts of Libya belonging to Cyrene, and visitors from Rome, both Jews and proselytes, Cretans and Arabians, we hear them telling in our own tongues the mighty works of God' (2:9-11). To speak the same language, to hear and to understand... Differences do exist, but the Spirit makes us understand the message of Jesus' resurrection, each in his or her own language.

"We have assembled here from 120 countries throughout the world, to celebrate the sovereign work of the Holy Spirit in the Church that occurred fifty years ago and started... an institution? No. An organization? No. A flood of grace, the flood of grace of the Catholic Charismatic Renewal. A work that was born... Catholic? No. It was born ecumenical! It was born ecumenical because it is the Holy Spirit who creates unity, and the same Spirit who granted the inspiration for this. It is important to read the works of Cardinal Suenens on this: it is very important!

"The coming of the Holy Spirit changes fearful men, enclosed behind shut doors, into courageous witnesses of Jesus. Peter, who had denied Jesus three times, filled with the power of the Holy Spirit, proclaims: 'Let all the house of Israel know assuredly that God has made him both Lord and Christ, this Jesus whom you crucified' (*Acts* 2:36). This is the profession of faith of every Christian! God has made both Lord and Christ that Jesus who was crucified. Are you all agreed on this profession of faith? It is ours, the same for all of us!

"The Scripture goes on to say: 'All who believed were together and had all things in common; and they sold their possessions and goods and distributed them to all, as any had need' (2:44-45). They sold them and they helped the poor. Some of them tried to be devious – we think of Ananias and Sapphira (there are always a few of them) – but all the believers, the great majority, helped one another. 'Day by day, attending the temple together and breaking bread in their homes, they partook of food with glad and generous hearts, praising God and having favour with all the people. And the Lord added to their number day by day those who were being saved' (2:46-47).

"The community kept growing and the Spirit was there to inspire this. I like to think of Philip, and how the angel told him: 'Take the road to Gaza and find that proselyte, the steward of Candace, Queen of Ethiopia. The man was a proselyte and he was reading Isaiah. Philip explained the scripture to him, proclaimed Jesus and the man converted. At a certain point, he said: "Here is some water: I want to be baptized."' It was the Spirit who led Philip to go there, and from the beginning it has been the Spirit who impels all the believers to proclaim the Lord.

Chapter Two: The Holy Fathers

"Today we have chosen to assemble here, in this place – as Pastor Traettino said – because here, during the persecutions, Christians were martyred for the entertainment of onlookers. Today there are more martyrs than then! Today there are more martyrs, Christians. Those who kill Christians do not ask them first: Are you Orthodox? Are you Catholic? Are you Evangelical? Are you Lutheran? Are you Calvinist? No. They ask if they are Christians, and when they say yes, they immediately slit their throats. Today there are more martyrs than in the early times. This is the ecumenism of blood. The witness of our martyrs today brings us together. In different parts of the world, Christian blood is being shed! Today Christian unity is more urgent than ever, Christians united by the power of the Holy Spirit, in prayer and in activity on behalf of the most vulnerable. To walk together, to [work] … together, to love one another, and together to seek to explain our differences, to come to agreement, but as we keep walking! If we stop walking, we will never come to agreement. So it is, because the Spirit wants us to keep walking.

"Fifty years of the Catholic Charismatic Renewal. A flood of grace of the Spirit! Why a flood of grace? Because it has no founder, no bylaws, no structure of governance. Clearly it has given rise to many expressions that, surely, are human works inspired by the Spirit, with various charisms, and all at the service of the Church. But before this flood of grace one cannot erect dikes, or put the Holy Spirit in a cage!

"Fifty years have gone by. At this age, our strength begins to decline. It is the halfway point of life – in my country, we call it *el cincuentazo* – when our wrinkles get deeper. Even if you cover them up, they are still there! Grey hairs start to show and we begin to forget things….

"Fifty years is a good time in life to stop and reflect. It is the time for reflection: the halfway point of life. And I would add this: it is the time to press forward with greater strength, leaving behind the accumulated dust of time, giving thanks for what we have received and looking ahead to new things, with trust in the working of the Holy Spirit!

"Pentecost gives birth to the Church. The Holy Spirit, the promise of the Father, of which Jesus spoke, is the One who makes the Church: the bride of the Book of Revelation, a single bride! Pastor Traettino said this: the Lord has *one* bride!

"The most precious gift that all of us have received is Baptism. And now the Spirit is leading us on this journey of conversion sweeping across the entire Christian world. It is one more reason why the Catholic Charismatic Renewal is a privileged place for pursuing the path to unity!

"This flood of grace is for the whole Church, not just for some, and none of us is the 'master' and the other servants. No. We are all servants of this flood of grace.

"Along with this experience, you constantly remind the Church of the power of prayer of praise. Praise that is the prayer of gratitude and thanksgiving for God's gracious love. Perhaps some people do not like this way of praying, but surely it is fully a part of the biblical tradition. Take the Psalms: David dances before the Ark of the Covenant, filled with exultation... And please, let us not fall into the attitude of Christians who have the 'Michol complex,' ashamed of the way David chose to praise God.

"Exultation, happiness, joy that is the fruit of the working of the Holy Spirit! Either a Christian experiences joy in his or her heart, or something is wrong. The joy of proclaiming the Good News of the Gospel!

"Jesus in the synagogue of Nazareth reads this passage of Isaiah: 'The Spirit of the Lord is upon me, because he has anointed me to preach good news to the poor. He has sent me to proclaim release to captives and recovering of sight to the blind, to set at liberty those who are oppressed, to proclaim the acceptable year of the Lord' (*Lk* 4:18-19; cf. *Is* 61:1-2). Good News, joyful news: do not forget this. Joyful news: the Christian message is always joyful.

"The third Malines document, 'Charismatic Renewal and Social Action,' written by Cardinal Suenens and Dom Helder Camara, states clearly that the charismatic renewal is also service to society, to humanity.

"*Baptism in the Holy Spirit, praise, social action.* The three things are inseparably linked. I can give deep thanks, but if I do not help those in need, it is not enough. 'There was not a needy person among them,' says the Book of Acts (4:34).

"We will be judged, not on our praise but on what we have done for Jesus. 'Lord, when did we do this to you? When you did it for one of these little ones, you did it to me' (cf. *Mt* 25:39-40).

"Dear brothers and sisters, my wish for you is that this will be a time of reflection, a time for remembering your origins. A time too, to leave behind everything motivated by self-concern. May it become a desire instead to listen to, and joyfully accept, the working of the Holy Spirit, who blows where and how he wills!

"I thank the Catholic Fraternity and ICCRS [International Catholic Charismatic Renewal Services] for organizing this Golden Jubilee, for this Vigil. And I thank each of the volunteers who make it possible, many of whom are present here. I wanted to greet the members of the office staff when I came, because I know how hard they have worked! And not for pay! They worked hard. Most of them are young people from different continents. May the Lord bless them all!

"I am particularly grateful that my request to you, two years ago, to give the worldwide Charismatic Renewal a single international service based here, has begun to take concrete shape in the acts of incorporation of this new single service. It is the first step, and others will follow, but soon the unity, the work of the Holy Spirit, will be a reality. 'I make all things new,' says the Lord (*Rev* 21:5).

"Thank you, Catholic Charismatic Renewal, for what you have given to the Church in these fifty years! The Church counts on you, on your fidelity to God's word, on your readiness to serve, and on your testimony of lives transformed by the Holy Spirit!

"To share baptism in the Holy Spirit with everyone in the Church, to praise the Lord unceasingly, to walk together with Christians of different Churches and Ecclesial Communities in prayer and activity on behalf of those in greatest need, to serve the poor and the sick. This is what the Church and the Pope expect from you, Catholic Charismatic Renewal, but also from everyone here: all of you who have become part of this flood of grace."[11]

And finally, as Pope Francis said during a Pentecost homily in 2013:

"The events that took place in Jerusalem almost two thousand years ago are not something far removed from us; they are events that affect us and become a lived experience in each of us."[12]

Catholic Charismatic Renewal Videos

The first QR code presents the opening song of the "Golden Jubilee of the Catholic Charismatic Renewal." As Pope Francis entered the arena, the song "Hosanna" greeted him. 50,000 attendees joyously sang along. Pure Holy Spirit energy poured forth from these charismatics—who welcomed our Holy Father.

Chapter Two: The Holy Fathers 43

The second QR code presents a well-crafted summary of the Catholic Charismatic Renewal. Many Catholics provide moving testimony about the transforming Holy Spirit EXPERIENCE. The video includes Pope Francis speaking at the Golden Jubilee.

YOUTUBE QR CODES

Catholic Charismatic Renewal and Pope Francis – HOSANNA

A Current of Grace The Catholic Charismatic Renewal Golden Jubilee

1. https://resurrectionparish.ca/files/docs/Papal_Quotes.pdf. Retrieval date: April 2, 2024.
2. Ibid.
3. Ibid.
4. Ibid.

5. Ibid.

6. Spiritual Renewal Services, Diocese of Norwich, CT.

7. https://resurrectionparish.ca/files/docs/Papal_Quotes.pdf. Retrieval date: April 2, 2024.

8. Ibid.

9. https://www.catholicnewsagency.com/news/27024/rejecting-holy-spirits-work-in-vatican-ii-is-foolish-pope-says. Retrieval date: April 22, 2024.

10. Reprinted from L'Osservatore, Romano, number 23, June 2014.

11. https://www.vatican.va/content/francesco/en/speeches/2017/june/documents/papa-francesco_20170603_veglia-pentecoste.html. Retrieval date: April 2, 2024.

12. https://www.vatican.va/content/francesco/en/homilies/2013/documents/papa-francesco_20130519_omelia-pentecoste.html. Retrieval date: April 8, 2024.

3
My Testimony

Dr. William Ayles interviewed me, Father Ray Introvigne, about my life, my ministry, and my experience with the Catholic Charismatic Renewal.

Talk to us about your family life, and what inspired you to become a priest.

My parents came from Italy in the early 1920s. They came from families that settled in different areas: one in New York and the other in Stafford Springs, Connecticut (CT). My mother, who had not yet come to Stafford Springs, arrived from Meriden on the trolley—which back then had its last stop in Stafford Springs. She found a job at a 'sweat shop' (factory). My dad was a mechanic at the Buick and Chevrolet dealership next door. They met and married in 1923 in Stafford Springs. They had three children before I was born.

They always attended Mass on Sundays. It seemed apparent to me that Mass was quite important to the immigrants coming from Italy—especially for the ladies. (Admittedly, I'm not sure of the depth of their faith.)

When mom was pregnant with me, dad brought my brother Joe, 8 years old, my sister Jean, 7 years old, and my sister Dolores, 4 years old, to Mass as usual. (The usual pastor wasn't celebrating Mass that morning.)

My family, unfortunately, was a little late in arriving—which happened so often with children. Then, to my father's shock, the church door was slammed in his face. I guess the usher tried to teach him a lesson. My father took this to mean God didn't want him, and he took the children home.

We didn't talk about God with my father. However, with my mother, we had to go to Mass with her—whether there was a foot of snow or pouring rain, we walked to church. We went to all the church novenas, missions, and other programs. Yet, so much damage was done in our lives because of the actions of one individual back in 1932.

I graduated from Stafford High School in Stafford Springs, in June 1950. My father, Joe Introvigne, still worked for the Buick and Chevrolet dealership. The owner had great respect for my dad and offered to send me for a two-year program at the General Motors Institute of Technology in Flint, Michigan, to prepare for a future in the automobile business. I was deciding between this or the funeral business that had been offered to me. I chose the General Motors Institute, and graduated August 8, 1952.

The Korean War had begun in 1950. Upon my graduation, the draft board leader told me if I didn't enlist by the coming Saturday, I would be drafted into the Army for three years. Knowing I was trained in internal-combustion engines—and most of the military and civilian planes were powered by internal-combustion engines—I enlisted in the U.S. Air Force for four years. I was sent to the Aircraft and Engine Mechanics School after basic training at Sheppard Air Force Base (AFB) in Wichita Falls, Texas, for a six-month course.

I did very well, and they sent me for a one-month course to train aircraft-engine mechanics. Upon finishing the course, I trained aircraft-engine mechanics for a year and a half at Sheppard AFB. I was then sent to Yokota AFB in Japan for the remainder of my enlistment. Upon my discharge in June 1956, my former pastor asked if I'd ever considered the priesthood. I said I hadn't because someone had once slammed the church door in my father's face. He said, 'Why don't you try it? And if it isn't for you, you'll never regret having tried.'

Before World War II, you couldn't enter seminary unless you attended a Catholic grammar school, a Catholic high school, a Catholic college, and a Catholic theology school. However, the Jesuit Fathers in Boston, Massachusetts, opened a school (in the 1940s/50s) for belated vocations called Saint Phillip Neri School. Additionally, they opened an overflow school on Newman Street in Boston at the School of Nursing for Boston College; we had our own space at the school.

In nine months, we covered four years of high-school Latin, two years of high-school French, three books of model English, a book on American literature, a book on English literature, and a book on religion. In June 1957, I completed the Saint Philip Neri coursework.

At this point, I received a call from Father Eusebe Menard of Canada. He had purchased a former alcohol-rehabilitation center in Cromwell, CT, that had been closed for 10 years. (This rehab center was quite exclusive, caring for clients like Bing Crosby and Judy Garland. Other greats were treated there as well.)

Father Eusebe asked me if I could come to help get the place ready for a seminary school to open that year. I arrived in August. As planned, it opened on September 7, 1957, with about 13 students in attendance (most of them from Canada).

At this time (July 1957), I received a letter from Bishop Bernard J. Flanagan, of the Norwich Diocese, directing me to attend Holy Apostles Seminary in Cromwell, beginning on September 7, 1957. (Connecticut is divided into three dioceses: Norwich, Bridgeport, and Hartford.)

I spent three years at Holy Apostles (as my college education), earning a Bachelor of Arts degree in Philosophy. I spent four years at Saint Bonaventure University, Christ the King

Seminary in Olean, New York, from September 1960 to May 1964, to earn a Master of Divinity degree.

Talk about your ordination in 1964, and the impact of Vatican II.

The Church ordained me May 7, 1964. I celebrated my first Mass in Latin, facing the wall. (All eight years of my educational training consisted of books in Latin, in theology. I was in one of the last classes to be ordained who followed the old order of Roman Catholic traditions.)

Vatican II would change the Mass: As of November 20, 1964, all Masses would be celebrated in the vernacular, the altar would be moved forward, and the priest would face the people. And with this change, this is how I felt:

> *The Mass became a beautiful 'meal' where the fullness of Jesus came to everyone attending, in the fullness of His Body, Soul, and Divinity. WOW!! What a powerful awesome Gift for all Catholic believers and lovers of our wonderful Father God, and His precious Son Jesus, and Their precious Holy Spirit... that each of us have... since our Baptism into His Holy Catholic Church—that our Lord built (Matt. 16:18). And to this day, I refer our brothers and sisters to what our Lord said in the Book of Revelation (3:20):*

> *"Listen! I (Jesus) stand at the door (of your heart) and knock. If you open the door (no handle on it), we (Father, Son & Holy Spirit) will come in (to your heart) and have dinner (spiritual intimacy) with you!! (Eucharist!)"*

Two of our priests (at Christ the King Seminary) were somewhat involved and interested in Vatican II and kept us in touch with what was going on. The Vatican II document went into effect six months after my ordination. (The November 20, 1964, document was the first of 16 Vatican II documents. Vatican II began with St. Pope John XXIII in 1962, and ran through 1965, with St. Pope Paul VI taking over in June 1963.)

My first assignment was a parish along the Connecticut shoreline, St. Agnes Church in Niantic. This document of the liturgy changed the way we approached our church community. For example, priests (of the Augustinian Order) offered, 'A Week of Prayer for Christian Unity.' And they published an ecumenical book that encouraged 'parish interfaith groups' to schedule an evening during that week for each church to host a community prayer service in each of the churches.

We began this type of prayer service the following year (1965), and did so with the following denominations: Episcopal, Lutheran Community Church, Assembly of God, even synagogues, etc. These prayer services did so much good—all thanks to St. Pope John XXIII having called Vatican II an 'Ecumenical Council.' We gathered for one week in each of the ecumenical churches to pray together and share together. I served as parochial vicar at St. Agnes for four years, and each year, we offered this prayer service.

From here, I was transferred to St. Joseph Church in Chester, but only for one year. Then I was sent to a church with a grammar school, Saint Sebastian Church in Middletown. We continued with the prayer service every year. The great effects of Vatican II were already being experienced in the Middletown area. There was a prayer group at Xavier Catholic High School. Many in the parish were asking me questions about Vatican II.

I should have attended the Xavier High School prayer meetings, but I decided to attend a prayer meeting in the Archdiocese of Hartford at Saint Maurice Church in New Britain. Thus, I could get answers, and be able to address any questions about Vatican II and the Charismatic Renewal.

I knew one of the priests who played the guitar at their prayer meeting. The gymnasium was filled—praising our Lord, with readings from Scripture, and a teaching, etc. This celebration continued for 1.5 hours. I was impressed. And I thought: I could answer anyone's questions about what unfolds at a prayer meeting!

Soon after, I experienced what I never experienced before: unmistakable, audible divine intervention. While celebrating Mass the following Sunday—right in the midst of my homily—I heard the voice of Jesus say,

'Ray, why aren't your people happy and joyful like the ones you were with Friday evening?'

Wow! I knew it was our Lord. This was the first time I'd ever heard our Lord speaking clearly to me. And He spoke into my ears during the main Sunday Mass at St. Sebastian Church!

That same afternoon, I went into the closed, dark church, and I cried by the Tabernacle, asking our Lord, 'What are You trying to tell me?' Nothing came. But deep down, I felt our Lord was telling me to return to the prayer meeting in New Britain—where no one would recognize me. (I didn't necessarily want anyone who knew me to see me because I was diving into something so new that I didn't quite know what to expect. Thus, I wanted to keep these 'surprises' to myself.)

After the welcome and prayer, the leader said, 'We are beginning a "Life in the Spirit" seminar tonight for eight weeks, 1.5 hours each night.'

When I asked about the seminar, they said it was a, 'head to heart experience,' or a 'personal relationship with Jesus!'

Well, I thought, 'I went to the seminary. I know all this.' See how my pride—above all—tried to get in the way and discourage me!? (Frankly, I never really intended to be a part of the Charismatic Renewal—but Jesus had other plans!)

I attended all eight sessions with other Catholic brothers and sisters.

And it changed my life and my priesthood. It's hard to explain. It was a 'falling in love with Jesus': a very deep feeling, an EXPERIENCE of God's love for me... for simple... ol' me. It's all a GIFT, from Jesus our Lord!

To this day—49 years later—that same peace and joy of heart is still there—even with all the crosses and temptations and poor choices and sins. Truly, as I reflect on it now, yes, it's all a gift. God is such an awesome God and Father.

At Vatican II, St. Pope John XXIII prayed for a NEW PENTECOST. And in 1967, several Duquesne University students received the Holy Spirit to overflowing and spoke in "new tongues." Tell us about the beginning of the Catholic Charismatic Renewal.

In February 1967, a few dozen students from Duquesne University in Pittsburgh, Pennsylvania, went to The Ark and the Dove retreat house. (As discussed in Chapter 1 of this book, the students received the Baptism of the Holy Spirit— the Renewal EXPERIENCE—overflowing in power.)

Upon returning to their university, the students then shared their EXPERIENCE with their teachers who were open to the Holy Spirit. They spoke of prayer and the 'Baptism in the Holy Spirit'—which was the 'Pentecost Gift' to the churches. This conversion experience changed these Catholics, from the inside out.

From that retreat at The Ark and the Dove, the 'Baptism of the Holy Spirit' and 'Speaking in New Tongues'—spread like wildfire throughout the world—even more powerfully in Third World countries.

Take us back to the 1970s and your trips to Franciscan University in Steubenville, Ohio, and what that experience meant to your ministry.

In 1975, the National Council of Catholic Bishops (NCCB) asked every bishop to send a representative to Franciscan University, as they wanted to appoint a national ad hoc committee. The NCCB sent five of their bishops to begin this process. These bishops would speak to the priests about their desire to form the Association of Diocesan Liaisons (a National Council of Diocesan Bishops Liaisons). This association would help the bishops in each diocese to shepherd the Catholic Charismatic Renewal.

Bishop Daniel Reilly sent me the letter and papers and asked me to attend. Upon my return, he asked me to help him shepherd the Catholic Charismatic Renewal in the Diocese of Norwich. He appointed me the first coordinator of prayer groups and then Director of Charismatic Renewal. This was in July of 1975—while I was parochial vicar at Saint Sebastian Church in Middletown (and a couple of months away from becoming pastor there).

Between 1975 and 1976 I made two trips to the Catholic Charismatic Priest retreat in Steubenville. A leadership team was formed, consisting of six leaders from around the country—and I was selected to be one of these priests (for a three-year term). To get it started, I was asked to be responsible for a national newsletter (we already offered a newsletter for our diocese).

At the 1976 Catholic Charismatic Priests' Conference, Father Michael Scanlon—president of Steubenville College—announced that Father Joseph Lange—a priest of the Order of St. LaSalle from Scranton, PA—would like to speak to any priest willing to offer a 'Six-day Parish Mission of Renewal and Evangelization' in their diocese. Father Lange planned to meet us after lunch at the tent. Of the 1000 priests in attendance, about 70 were interested.

Father Lange gave a powerful and convincing talk. In conclusion, he said, 'Let me know [your intentions]. If yes, plan to fly to Scranton in two weeks. We will prepare you and provide you with all the materials to offer these missions.'

About twenty priests registered. This was an awesome opportunity: one week with Father Joe Lange, learning from him. It proved to be one of the greatest gifts of my life and priesthood; it was July 1976.

Upon returning to my parish, I thought, 'How will the Holy Spirit be able to place this into practice?'

And, 'Now what could "simple me" do with this gift?'

Nothing came to mind: August, September, October, and November passed, and nothing yet was evident. Then came Advent. Each year, I was responsible for an Advent program for the parish. Usually fifteen to twenty parishioners would attend.

I asked my pastor, Father Zenon Smilga, Ph.D., if I could offer this 'Six-day Parish Mission of Renewal and Evangelization.' (For me, this seminar was a true gift of Vatican II, which had ended only eleven years earlier.)

Father Smilga gave me the green light, and we advertised the program. The church was *filled* each night.

After the third night, the pastor asked me, 'What are you going to do with these people after the mission?'

I said, 'You are the pastor, Father, it's up to you to determine what to do from here. I only offered this Advent program!'

He said, 'I'm going to ask all those who are interested to share on where to go from here, and to come next Thursday to a meeting—and you, Father Ray, will conduct the meeting!'

About 100 people came. We shared our thoughts, and most favored having a prayer group—which began that evening. God is good... all the time!

During the following seven years, I was able—and privileged—to offer 24 of these Six-day Parish of Mission Renewal and Evangelization missions.

At this time (1985), Bishop Reilly asked me to pastor St. John Church in Old Saybrook. He intended to reopen a closed school and told me to continue our work with the Charismatic Renewal.

How did your bishop respond to your Ohio experience?

It was received very well by Bishop Reilly. He had accepted Vatican II and what it stood for: renewing the Church and its people. He also was on board with the approval and encouragement given by The United States Conference of Catholic Bishops. The USCCB started The National Diocesan Association of Liaisons that year—and this body still ministers in the Church.

Bring us back to when you first spoke in "new tongues" (the Holy Spirit Language).

I was in awe of our awesome Lord and Savior—for His grace and favor.

For God to give me this gift of prayer—in God's language (of the Holy Spirit)—and for Him to make it so easy to do so, showed me that God could give this new language to anyone and everyone in the Church of Christ! All our brothers and sisters in Christ could speak forth this gift... if they choose to do so. We make the decisions!

Looking back 2000 years, on the day of Pentecost, the disciples spoke (and prayed) in tongues. God testified to the world that His salvation through Christ is backed up by supernatural power—including gifts of the Holy Spirit. And He continues to demonstrate His power through His gifts to this very day! Amen!

Speaking in New Tongues

One gift of the Holy Spirit is the language of the Holy Spirit: speaking in new tongues. It is Christ's irrefutable, divine sign that testifies to the indwelling presence of the Holy Spirit.

Now, let me tell you about the Scriptures that continue to mean so much to me regarding this beautiful gift of new tongues. You deserve to understand what our Lord and His apostles revealed to us.

The Apostle Paul

Paul said when we speak in the Holy Spirit language, we speak mysteries unto our God:

"For those who speak in a tongue do not speak to other people but to God; for nobody understands them, since they are speaking mysteries in the Spirit" (1 Cor. 14:2).

And Paul revealed to us the will of the Holy Spirit: "I would like all of you to speak in tongues" (1 Cor. 14:5). This gift of divine tongues is not designed to be limited, but rather, universal—for the universal Church of Christ.

Paul also told us he followed the will of the Holy Spirit: "I thank God that I speak in tongues more than all of you" (1 Cor. 14:18). And Paul said, "Be imitators of me, as I am of Christ" (1 Cor. 11:1). Whom shall we follow? Paul!

Our Dear Lord

And our dear Lord told us this: "And these signs will accompany those who believe: by using my name... they will speak in new tongues" (Mark 16:17).

Christ's prophecy came to pass on the day of Pentecost. On that day, He gave a visual sign for all to see: flaming tongues of fire. As Luke recorded:

> "Divided tongues, as of fire, appeared among them, and a tongue rested on each of them. All of them were filled with the Holy Spirit and began to speak in other languages, as the Spirit gave them ability" (Acts 2:3, 4).

The Holy Spirit placed a vision of a "tongue" (of all things) over the (about) 120 disciples. With their new tongues they spoke "mysteries"—speaking of God's power. Listen to what the crowd said:

> "[I]n our own languages we hear them speaking about God's deeds of power" (Acts 2:11).

This Holy Spirit language is a supernatural sign granted to us. And this Holy Spirit language is perfect. Thus, we offer unto our God perfect praise! Wouldn't you like to do what the disciples did?!

Praying and Singing in Tongues

Paul said:

> "I will pray with the spirit, but I will pray with the mind also; I will sing praise with the spirit, but I will sing praise with the mind also" (1 Cor. 14:15).

Let us be an imitator of Paul: As he spoke, prayed, and sang in new tongues, so can you.

Your Gift of New Tongues

On Pentecost, when our Lord baptized His apostles with the Holy Spirit, they spoke in the language of the Spirit. Please know this: The mechanics of speech to speak in your Holy Spirit language are identical to the mechanics of speech for your native language.

God will not force you to speak in a divine language by opening your mouth. You push air through your throat; you move your tongue and lips to form words (that sound like syllables). He will fill it with prayer tongues. Your Holy Spirit language is of the Spirit (which is already within you). As Paul revealed to us, "if I pray in a tongue, my spirit prays" (1 Cor. 14:14).

Speaking in your gifted, divine language sounds like syllables strung together in your native language. When we desire to pray in our divine language, we consciously think of our Lord and speak to Him. Or we can sing in our spiritual language in joyful exaltation!

To take this a step further, we all 'speak *with* our tongues' in our everyday speech. It's automatic. We know this. Now, put yourself in the disciples' sandals. They made a choice: They chose to follow and believe their Lord. And, upon receiving their Holy Spirit EXPERIENCE, *all* the disciples moved their 'tongues' and mouths as they always did, but they did so in their gifted language. The Holy Spirit language simply flowed out from them. In other words, if you have the Holy Spirit within, you also have the Holy Spirit language within.

Trust your Lord. Pray. And with your heart-felt humility, yield to the Holy Spirit. Speak. And guess what? Sounds and syllables will slowly develop (i.e., "la – la, la – ma," etc.). It may sound foreign to you—because it is! It's heavenly!

Start humming or singing a familiar song and let the Holy Spirit teach you how to do so in your divine language. Our Lord said our Holy Spirit will guide us into the truth. If we live by the Spirit, we will be guided by the Spirit. The Spirit guides us, and gives us His language, but please know you are in complete control of this gift: You decide when to speak it forth.

We are blessed and invited to ask for and accept this gift of Pentecost—simply decide... Yes! And then, why not order the "Life in the Spirit" video and let the original Duquesne students guide you into speaking forth this blessed gift?!

Now, consider what our Lord revealed to His apostles:

> "You did not choose me but I chose you [put your name here]. And I appointed you to go and bear fruit, fruit that

will last, so that the Father will give you whatever you ask him in my name" (John 15:16).

Ask. Seek. Pray. Your prayer life is your lifeline to Heaven. Bear Fruit. You can expect your divine prayer language to develop over time. Truly, it's part of the Church's Baptismal gifts. God is at work within you!

Many books are available expounding upon this gift of the Holy Spirit language[1]—including *What is Going On* By Monsignor Vincent M. Walsh.

Monsignor Vincent M. Walsh

I would like to call your attention to Monsignor Vincent M. Walsh and the wonderful book he wrote, *What is Going On*. Like me, he EXPERIENCED the Baptism of the Holy Spirit. Listen to his comforting and encouraging words on the gift of 'prayer tongues':

> "The best way to explain prayer tongues is the following: Normal human speech involves three faculties – the will (to choose to speak), the intellect (to choose the words [that sound like syllables]) and the lips (to form the sound waves). Praying in tongues involves only the will (the decision to speak) and the lips (the sounds of being formed). No intellect is used while praying in tongues because the words of prayer are given by the Holy Spirit. (My own prayer tongues is a French spoken many centuries ago which have been translated by a French nurse, Jeanine Nichols.)

"Once yielded to, the experience of praying in tongues is permanent, able to be used whenever the person wishes. (Like learning to ride a bike.) Praying in tongues is extremely important. Because the intellect is free, the spirit can lift the person's mind to God in mental prayer."[2]

Now, listen to Monsignor Walsh elaborate on this subject:

"The Pentecostal package comes in three parts:
1) Baptism of the Spirit
2) Praying in tongues
3) Spiritual gifts (or charisms)

"The first two are personal for the individual's own sanctification and can be received by all if sound teaching and practice are present.

"The spiritual gifts are distributed by the Holy Spirit and are received according to the Spirit's decision of how He wants the person to serve. These spiritual gifts (charisms) are for the good of others and the Church. Paul gives the classic list of nine basic charisms (1 Cor. 12:7-11) which are usually divided into three groups.

A) Word gifts: tongues, interpretation of tongues and prophecy
B) Power gifts: healing, miracles and faith (that moves mountains)
C) Intellectual gifts: discernment of spirits, word of wisdom and word of knowledge.

"The Pentecostal Community

"Pentecostal experiences don't float in the air like radio waves. The Spirit places His gifts in persons and these persons have to come together. According to St. Paul, the Spirit promises the fullness of gifts only to the Pentecostal community. To each, the Spirit distributes a different gift, but only to the whole community does He promise all the gifts.

"Pentecostalism is a flame and when the logs are separated, the flame dies out. Only when people come together is the flame alive and powerful. Coming together is the secret."[3]

For me and my gift, I still pray with – and use and enjoy – this Holy Spirit language of "new tongues" every day. In the car, I don't play the radio or CDs, but rather, I enjoy praying the Rosary/chaplet, and singing in tongues… singing songs of praise and worship—loving our God… with a heart overflowing with joy!

Our Dear Lord

And now, I ask that you place your trust in our Lord and His comforting words:

"And remember, I am with you always, to the end of the age" (Matt. 28:20).

Jesus is on our side—now and forever.

How did your relationship with our Lord Jesus Christ change?

The best way for me to explain what happened is this:

> *It was a powerful change from my head to my heart. Truly, it was 'a falling in love, so to speak, with Jesus'—in a heartfelt way. Before this, it was mostly from my mind. Then, the Holy Spirit changed all that: "The joy of the Lord is your strength!"*4

We can know someone. We can know theology and teach it from the head. However, sooner or later we need a 'conversion experience' to deeply touch our hearts! For me, it was the *Cursillo* (which means a 'short course'). It is a retreat I participated in two years after my ordination. And I attended a Life in the Spirit seminar eleven years after ordination. (The Life in the Spirit seminar is called 'A Packaged Pentecost Experience.')

> *These 'conversion experiences' forever changed my life, my priesthood, and my personal relationship with my Lord. The Catholic Charismatic Renewal opened a door to the 'grace and favor' of God's gifts like never before!*

What changed for you personally, and in your ministry, and with Scripture?

We all need to know this: The Holy Spirit was an EXPERIENCE (on Pentecost) before becoming a doctrine. It is still meant to be an EXPERIENCE.

Chapter Three: My Testimony

For me, praise and worship gatherings came ALIVE—just like we read in Psalm 150:

> "Praise the LORD!
> Praise God in his sanctuary; praise him in his mighty firmament!
> Praise him for his mighty deeds; praise him according to his surpassing greatness!
> Praise him with trumpet sound; praise him with lute and harp!
> Praise him with tambourine and dance; praise him with strings and pipe!
> Praise him with clanging cymbals; praise him with loud clashing cymbals!
> Let everything that breathes praise the LORD!
> Praise the LORD!"

One week after being baptized in the Holy Spirit, this is what I experienced:

- When I came out to celebrate Mass, it came alive in a powerful way! (I had been a priest for eleven years at this point.)
- The Bible came alive! Prior to the Holy Spirit Baptism EXPERIENCE, I taught from the head; now, I taught from the heart.
- My prayer life came alive! Prayer no longer felt like an obligation, but rather, I enjoyed prayer! I felt a deep, personal connection with Jesus.

These graces and blessings are still with me at 92 years *young*—49 years later. I'm still ministering. I continue to host various seminars—including 'A.C.T.S.' ... I haven't retired.

Talk to us about the "A.C.T.S." seminars. What do you ask of our bishops and priests?

"A.C.T.S." stands for "Adoration, Community, Theology, Service."

Back in 2004, our Immaculata Retreat House in Willimantic was connected with priests in Texas who started A.C.T.S. The Texas priests wanted to come up to Connecticut and bring us the A.C.T.S. seminar. Tragically, they couldn't find a parish, or a pastor, interested. When I was asked, I was excited because I had made a Cursillo in 1966.

In 1966, I had only been a priest for two years. At that time I noticed those in my area who had attended a Cursillo were different: joyful, kind, thoughtful, helpful, etc. It deeply touched me. I felt inspired to attend one.

St. Peter's Church in Hartford offered it. WOW! It was an eye-opening experience in 'Christian Living': loving God with your heart, soul, mind, and strength, and loving (appreciating) your brothers and sisters in Christ—regardless of race, color, or creed! All who attended this Cursillo were overwhelmingly blessed.

A.C.T.S. adds to the Cursillo, 'to help renew the Parish and the Church' (as children of God, part of God's divine family). And this is what I would like every Catholic parishioner to know:

> *A.C.T.S. and Cursillo are movements within the Church to give life to the essential Christian truths. During a weekend retreat, participants will live, learn and worship together. And it leads one into a 'conversion experience.' This experience is offered on a silver platter for all to embrace—including bishops, priests, deacons, laity, etc. This*

Chapter Three: My Testimony

A.C.T.S. retreat has the purpose of helping the parish come alive.

When men and women attend, they are touched so deeply that they go out and try to get their husbands, wives, relatives, friends, employers, etc. to go. It's said to be one of the 'best evangelization tools available to us' because those who attended became the best evangelizers. They get involved in their churches, as well.

If only the bishops and priests would attend one seminar (one A.C.T.S. retreat, or one Cursillo) to EXPERIENCE the Holy Spirit in that deeper way. This way, they could inform their own flock regarding the possibilities that await. It's that simple!

Personally, I very much enjoyed taking "Life in the Spirit" seminars with you. Talk to us about this seminar and its status.

As charismatic priests, we teach our people about the Holy Spirit Baptism. Then, we encourage them to attend a Life in the Spirit seminar—and do so prayerfully. And do so with an open mind and heart.

And the result? They are baptized in the Holy Spirit, receiving a Pentecost EXPERIENCE. From here, hopefully they will attend a weekly prayer meeting. The foundation for Life in the Spirit seminars began with Vatican II.

Today, our renewal ministry is now under the Office of Faith Events for the nine ministries in the Norwich Diocese. Mrs. Andrea Hoisl is the director. And she has brought forth a four-week seminar, 'Awakening to the Holy Spirit.' We pray and believe that 'Awakening' will baptize those who come with open minds and hearts (as is the case with A.C.T.S.).

I should note that—in the world—the Catholic Charismatic Renewal remains vibrant, especially in Third World countries. Really, we are spoiled in our country (America). We have so many blessings—which make us rich in such a way that God isn't appreciated as much. However, our dear Lord keeps loving us and calling us.

Talk to us about the Charismatic Renewal in the Church.

All our modern-day popes encouraged us to embrace Vatican II, the Charismatic Renewal, and Life in the Spirit seminars.

Yet you may ask, 'Why isn't the Renewal flourishing in the Church today?'

In my opinion, the transforming experience that Vatican II brought forth didn't thoroughly make its way down through the 'ranks' of the Church: cardinals, archbishops, bishops, priests, apostolic delegates, and theologians didn't necessarily embrace the Renewal.

It's important for us to understand that if bishops hold back, then (typically) their priests hold back—and they don't embrace the Renewal in Vatican II. In some cases, older priests just don't want to make any changes in their ministry. Others are simply content with their existing knowledge—and have no interest in expanding into the Renewal.

Thank God, there were bishops, priests, and laity who did embrace the work of the Holy Spirit—and the Renewal in those early days blossomed.

Worldwide Catholic Priest Retreat

In October 1984, the Vatican hosted a Worldwide Catholic Priest Retreat at the St. Pope Paul VI Audience Hall in Rome; 80 bishops and 6000 priests came together as one to hear about the theme: 'God's Call to Holiness, God's First Call to Priests Today.'

Many of us at the retreat embraced the Renewal. We praised and worshiped God in our native languages and in our Holy Spirit languages. The singing and praising of our dear Lord was awesome! *Praise God* for this divine opportunity to live the glory of this Renewal with fellow liaisons from around the world.

Yet, while praising God, it was clear that not all bishops and priests had embraced the Charismatic Renewal. And listen to this: We (who did embrace the Renewal) were actually asked to tone down our praise and worship. We did. We respected their request. We understood a fundamental truth: 'Love people for where they are and not where you expect or desire they would be!' At the retreat—above all—we were there to share the love of Christ.

There were two important architects of the retreat: Fr. Tom Forrest and Leon Joseph Cardinal Suenens. Both men fully supported the Catholic Charismatic Renewal. Cardinal Suenens—a principal architect of Vatican II—played an active role in fostering various lay movements in the Catholic Church, including Life in the Spirit seminars and the Legion of Mary.

During the retreat, Cardinal Suenens spoke to us with such love, and with such moving words. His words still speak volumes to us today... and this is what He shared with us:

"When Christ said, 'If anyone thirsts let him come to me; let him drink who believes in me,' the text itself adds that he was referring to his promise of the Holy Spirit. What especially interests me is how the evangelist [John] explains that these words were 'cried out' by Christ (Jn. 7:37–39). Since it is not common to read in the Gospels about Jesus crying out this way, there must be a very special significance to the promise he is making.

"Today we find ourselves not in Jerusalem but here in Rome. The cry of the Lord, nevertheless, remains the same. With the words, 'Come to me and I will give you to drink,' Jesus is telling us that, if we go to him, he will give us the fullness of his Holy Spirit. This is a promise for all of us, and the desire to see it fulfilled is the reason we are here today."[5]

My Diocese

For me—as a liaison from America—I desired to bring this excitement back to my parishioners.

Now, let me share my own Renewal Experience in my diocese. My first bishop, Daniel Reilly, was a best friend of Father John Randall (who was a pioneer of the Renewal from the beginning). They went through the seminary together—and both were from Providence, Rhode Island. Father John received a doctorate in Scripture. Bishop Reilly received a doctorate in Theology.

Bishop Reilly fully supported me and the renewal. He sent out letters, endorsing and encouraging the Catholic Charismatic Renewal. And he appointed Judith Hughes as Associate Coordinator of our Diocesan Catholic Charismatic Renewal in Old Saybrook, to strengthen our renewal and parish activities.

Years later, in 1999, Bishop Daniel Hart assigned me to another parish. With this responsibility, I needed help shepherding the renewal. Thankfully, Bishop Hart appointed Judith Hughes as Co-director of our Diocesan Catholic Charismatic Renewal ministry to handle the volume of demands relative to this enjoyable, blossoming ministry of Vatican II, including the following:

- Personal witnesses
- Charismatic programs (including our publication, *The Holy Spirit Digest*)
- Life in the Spirit seminars
- Charismatic Masses and healing services
- Holy Spirit breakfasts, lunches and dinners with nationally renowned speakers
- Prayer groups and training sessions for leaders (reaching 34 prayer groups around the diocese out of 70 parishes)
- 'Companions of the Cross': A charismatic religious community—founded by Fr. Bob Bedard—composed of priests and seminarians that minister in parishes and schools across Canada and America with their charism of evangelization and charismatic worship.
- National courses, including the following:

    - *Little Rock Scripture Study—Applying the Bible to Daily Life*
    - Healing Course
    - *Unbound*: a practical guide (book) to deliverance[6]

These renewal movements—along with others (like A.C.T.S. and Awakening)—are the greatest gifts of Vatican II!

We reached so many Catholics through these inspired efforts. I can testify that these Catholics hungered and thirsted for a closer walk with our Lord; they sought the truth of the Holy Spirit Renewal: a New Pentecost in their hearts. Looking back in time, I can honestly say that this renewal work 'took off' thanks to the diligent efforts of Judith Hughes, along with countless secretaries and volunteers.

I thank God for Bishop Reilly; he fully supported our renewal work. And I'm thankful for the two bishops who followed Bishop Reilly; each gave us a free hand to continue our efforts. Thank you, Jesus! Thank you, Holy Spirit!

Yet, looking back in time, I am saddened to say this: 'Compared to the time of Bishop Reilly, there has been a great drop off in those who desire Renewal programs and correspondence.' (Bishop Reilly appointed me Director of Charismatic Renewal in September 1976.)

Today, an honest assessment of the Catholic Charismatic Renewal yields a sobering thought: 'How many took advantage of spiritual benefits of the Renewal? Not enough... unfortunately! The proof is in the pudding!'

Our Priests, Our Shepherds

Now, I'd like to switch the subject to our priests who don't embrace the Catholic Charismatic Renewal—and ask a few honest questions.

> Why is it that our seminary-driven spirituality excludes the Holy Spirit EXPERIENCE of the Catholic Charismatic Renewal?

What can possibly be gained by dismissing the Holy Spirit EXPERIENCE as handed to us by the apostles and advocated by all our modern-day Holy Fathers?

It is a personal choice... yes?

Is not the Holy Spirit EXPERIENCE a gift from our Lord for our Holy Catholic Church?
Did not our Lord and Savior instruct His apostles that they would become witnesses unto all the Earth—*after receiving the baptism of the Holy Spirit, which included fulfilling His prophecy of speaking in new tongues?*

Tragically, as we know, our bishops failed to appoint liaisons to help them shepherd the Renewal and, thus, the Renewal hasn't taken hold or blossomed in dioceses across the country the way it could have.

Frankly, Pope Francis was so disappointed that the charisms of Pentecost and our Renewal were not overwhelmingly appreciated and accepted – or at least tried – that he called back to Rome leaders of the various Renewal Movements. His goal is to repackage this awesome 'Conversion Experience' (the Pentecost charism [gift].) We are waiting now for the results!

Reflection

Here we are in 2025!

To think, the seeds of our Catholic Holy Spirit Renewal extend all the way back to 1895! That is when Blessed Sister Elena began writing to Pope Leo XIII calling for renewed preaching on the Holy Spirit.

Monsignor Vincent M. Walsh speaks of this in his book, *What is Going On*:

> "Pope Leo responded to Elena's letters by publishing *Provida Matris Caritate* (The Provident Charity of a Mother) asking for a solemn novena between the Ascension and Pentecost throughout the Church. This was not enough, Sister Elena prodded the Pope through her spiritual guide. Pope Leo wrote his famous encyclical on the Holy Spirit, *Divinum Illud Munus* ("That Divine Gift"). The encyclical was excellent but the response from the Church was poor.
>
> "Possibly even more important at the insistence of Blessed Elena, he dedicated the 20th Century to the Holy Spirit, invoking on January 1, 1901 the *Veni Creator Spiritus* ("Come Holy Spirit") upon the whole world."[7]

Thank God, in 1967, our Lord renewed the Church with His Holy Spirit. Today, after decades of the Catholic Charismatic Renewal, this is what I would like for you to know: There is one Holy Spirit, and one true Church that Christ set up, and He has bestowed upon the Church this beautiful blessing of the Holy Spirit Renewal.

He has given us countless invitations in Scripture – for us – to participate in this Renewal EXPERIENCE. But please know this: He leaves it up to us to accept His invitations!

As Paul exhorted us: "pursue love and strive for the spiritual gifts" (1 Cor. 14:1).

And as our Lord exhorted us: "strive first for the kingdom of God and his righteousness, and all these things will be given to you as well" (Matt. 6:33).

Please share your closing thoughts with us.

God created us for Himself, to know, to love and serve Him with all our hearts and with all our souls, and with all our minds. And to love our neighbors as ourselves (Matthew 22:37–39). He created us to embrace Him, to find our happinesses and successes, and embrace Him during our sadnesses and failures.

There are only two main powers: good and evil. There is our God who is on our side. And there is our enemy, Satan, who looks to deceive us. Don't be deceived by the enticing words of those who would lead us astray—away from our Lord. The words of our Lord Jesus Christ ground us, inspire us, and direct us.

Let us look back to the words of Jesus, that we may move forward in our lives!

On the very day of His Ascension, Jesus promised His disciples they would be baptized with the Holy Spirit. He promised the Holy Spirit would overflow in power.

This is the historical record:

> "While staying with them, he [Jesus] ordered them not to leave Jerusalem, but to wait there for the promise of the Father. 'This,' he said, 'is what you have heard from me; for John baptized with water, but you will be baptized with the Holy Spirit not many days from now.'... '[Y]ou will receive power when the Holy Spirit has come upon you; and you will be my witnesses in Jerusalem, in all Judea and Samaria, and to the ends of the earth'" (Acts 1:4, 5, 8).

As we heard in Chapter 1 (from David Mangan), the Greek word for 'power' is where we get the word 'dynamite.' Just like the disciples, today, we 'wait' for His promise, and we receive

His dynamite. How? It is by our expectation to receive from our Lord; it is by our faith and prayer—and it is by seeking His will that we receive from Him.

Attend a retreat with an open mindset, and with an expectant heart, and with expectant faith. And let me suggest to you what the Duquesne students did: Please read the first four chapters of the Book of Acts.

And yes, let everyone of us Praise the Lord! Let us offer Him perfect praise—with our Holy Spirit language. Let us celebrate our Creator! "Take delight in the Lord and he will give you the desires of your heart" (Ps. 37:4).

Now, let me tell you how I really feel about all this. Psalm 40:3 says it best:

"He put a new song [tongues] in my mouth
[so I now speak from an abundance of joy in my heart],
a song of praise [and worship] to our God.
"Many [like you] will see and fear,
and put their trust in the Lord."

In closing, I'd like to share what our God told the prophet Jeremiah. I ask that you put yourself in Jeremiah's sandals.

"For surely I [God] know the plans I have for you [put your name here], says the Lord, plans for your welfare and not for harm, to give you a future with hope. Then when you call upon me and come and pray to me, I will hear you. When you search for me, you will find me; if you seek me with all your heart, I will let you find me, says the Lord, and I will restore your fortunes [change your circumstances]" (Jer. 29:11–14).

May God bless you abundantly as you EXPERIENCE Your Renewal!

WCAT Radio

I conclude My Testimony by recommending five WCAT Radio shows that explore the Catholic Charismatic Renewal. The WCAT Radio channel is 'Treasures in Heaven,' and the host is the same gentlemen who interviewed me, Dr. William Ayles.

HTTPS://WCATRADIO.COM/TREASURESINHEAVEN/
The episodes are as follows: 42, 43, 45, 46, 47.

    1. Of the many books available on the subject, there is one book we recommend you start with: *A Personal Relationship with Jesus*. This wonderful book was written by a dear friend of ours (who has since gone to be with the Lord), Father Bill McCarthy, M.S.A. (Father Bill asked me [Father Ray] to write the Foreword of the book, and I was honored to do so.) This book is available at Holy Apostles Seminary and College, 33 Prospect Hill Road, Cromwell, CT 06416. (860) 632-3010. A second book is by Monsignor Vincent M. Walsh: *What is Going On*. It is available on Amazon.

    2. Monsignor Vincent M. Walsh, *What is Going On* (Wynnewood, PA: Key of David Publications, 1995), pp. 4, 5.

    3. Monsignor Vincent M. Walsh, *What is Going On*, pp. 7, 8.

    4. Nehemiah 8:10.

    5. "Be Holy: God's First Call to Priests Today," Retreat Guide, (1984).

    6. *UnBound* was written by Neil Lozano. It is available at Heart of the Father Ministries, P.O. Box 905, Ardmore, PA 19003. (610) 952-3019.

7. Monsignor Vincent M. Walsh, *What is Going On*, pp. 158, 159.

Act Two

4
Our Lord

> "I will ask the Father, and he will give you another Advocate, to be with you forever. This is the Spirit of truth, whom the world cannot receive, because it neither sees him nor knows him. You know him, because he abides with you, and he will be in you."
>
> —Christ (John 14:16, 17)

How important are prophecies given by the Son of God on the day of His Ascension to the right hand of God?

Ascension Day

Just prior to His Ascension into Heaven, the risen Christ spoke to His disciples about the sign of "new tongues":

> "'[T]hese signs will accompany those who believe: ... they will speak in new tongues.'... So then the Lord Jesus, after he had spoken to them, was taken up into heaven and sat down at the right hand of God. And they went out and proclaimed the good news everywhere, while the Lord worked with them and confirmed the message by the signs that accompanied it" (Mark 16:17, 19, 20).

As Christ lifted off to the clouds, the apostles stood staring into Heaven with the assurance their Lord would fulfill His prophecies. Ten days after His Ascension, came the day of Pentecost. And on that day, Christ fulfilled His promises: He baptized His disciples with the Holy Spirit—and the divine signs followed.

Our Lord gave His Church a new "tongue": the divine language of our Holy Spirit.

We will see this supernatural sign unfold in the coming chapters. But before we explore how this sign unfolded in the early Church, we need to know what Christ Himself said about the Holy Spirit. Then, we will know we are standing on solid ground. Therefore, let us answer a question: What did our Lord reveal to us about the Holy Spirit during His ministry?

Christ's Ministry

Christ handed us sound doctrine regarding the Holy Spirit all throughout His ministry.

He spoke to a temple authority.
He spoke to a Samaritan woman at a well.
He issued a prophecy during a Jewish holy festival.
And He issued several prophecies during The Last Supper.

A Temple Authority

"Now there was a Pharisee named Nicodemus, a leader of the Jews. He came to Jesus by night and said to him, 'Rabbi, we know that you are a teacher who has come from God; for no one can do these signs that you do apart from the presence of God.' Jesus answered him, 'Very truly, I tell you, no one can see the kingdom of God without being born from above.' Nicodemus said to him, 'How

can anyone be born after having grown old? Can one enter a second time into the mother's womb and be born?' Jesus answered, 'Very truly, I tell you, no one can enter the kingdom of God without being born of water and Spirit. What is born of the flesh is flesh, and what is born of the Spirit is spirit. Do not be astonished that I said to you, "You must be born from above." The wind blows where it chooses, and you hear the sound of it, but you do not know where it comes from or where it goes. So it is with everyone who is born of the Spirit.'... 'For God so loved the world that he gave his only Son, so that everyone who believes in him may not perish but may have eternal life. Indeed, God did not send the Son into the world to condemn the world, but in order that the world might be saved through him'" (John 3:1–8, 16, 17).

Woman at the Well

During His time in the Holy Land, Jesus introduced us to the concept of worshiping God in the Spirit and in truth. And this is what Christ revealed to a Samaritan woman—while the two were at a well.

She drew water, but Jesus told her about "living water":

"A Samaritan woman came to draw water, and Jesus said to her, 'Give me a drink.' (His disciples had gone to the city to buy food.) The Samaritan woman said to him, 'How is it that you, a Jew, ask a drink of me, a woman of Samaria?' (Jews do not share things in common with Samaritans.) Jesus answered her, 'If you knew the gift of God, and who it is that is saying to you, "Give me a drink," you would have asked him, and he would have given you living water'" (John 4:7–10).

"The woman said to him, 'Sir, you have no bucket, and the well is deep. Where do you get that living water? Are you greater than our ancestor Jacob, who gave us the well, and with his sons and his flocks drank from it?' Jesus said to her, 'Everyone who drinks of this water will be thirsty again, but those who drink of the water that I will give them will never be thirsty. The water that I will give will become in them a spring of water gushing up to eternal life.' The woman said to him, 'Sir, give me this water, so that I may never be thirsty or have to keep coming here to draw water'" (John 4:11–15).

Our Lord revealed what we need to know: Those of us who thirst for the truth will be satisfied. How? The Holy Spirit is the answer. Through Christ, we are filled with living water that is *everlasting* living water; the Holy Spirit is eternal. And this is how our eternal life springs forth: the eternal Spirit our Lord gives us.

No wonder the Samaritan woman wanted this living water. Now, let us read what Jesus explained to the woman:

"Jesus said to her, 'Woman, believe me, the hour is coming when you will worship the Father neither on this mountain nor in Jerusalem.... But the hour is coming, and is now here, when the true worshipers will worship the Father in spirit and truth, for the Father seeks such as these to

> worship him. God is spirit, and those who worship him must worship in spirit and truth.' The woman said to him, 'I know that Messiah is coming' (who is called Christ). 'When he comes, he will proclaim all things to us.' Jesus said to her, 'I am he, the one who is speaking to you'" (John 4:21, 23–26).

Jesus revealed who He is: the Messiah, our Savior, the Anointed One of God. And all who hear the truth hear His voice.

Jesus told the woman that worshiping God would no longer be confined to the temple in Jerusalem, but rather, worship of our Creator would be by the same Holy Spirit with which we are baptized.

A Holy Festival

As Jesus continued ministering among the people, He attended a holy festival. At this Jewish festival, Christ issued a prophecy like what He gave to the Samaritan woman: The power of the Holy Spirit would overflow like water.

> "Now the Jewish festival of Booths was near.... On the last day of the festival, the great day, while Jesus was standing there, he cried out, 'Let anyone who is thirsty come to me, and let the one who believes in me drink. As the scripture has said, "Out of the believer's heart shall flow rivers of living water."' Now he said this about the Spirit, which believers in him were to receive; for as yet there was no Spirit, because Jesus was not yet glorified" (John 7:2, 37–39).

At the time of this holy festival, Christ was not yet glorified. (He would be glorified after His Ascension to the Father.)

After His glorification, Christ poured out "living water": the Holy Spirit. Then, "rivers of living water" spiritually cleansed His disciples—and overflowed in spiritual power. How? How does the Holy Spirit overflow in power?

Consider how Christ prophesied we would receive "living water." What does it mean to "receive"?

"Receive" is the Greek word *Lambano*—which denotes an "objective reception."[1] In other words, the living water is designed to fill us, and in addition, overflow out of us—in demonstrated power (which includes divine gifts); this includes the gift of speaking in the language of the Holy Spirit.

Let us—in our day—thirst for this living water to overflow in power. Let us thirst for the renewing power of the Holy Spirit EXPERIENCE.

The Last Supper

At The Last Supper, our Lord revealed to His apostles several prophecies (that we can take to heart):

> **"I will ask the Father, and he will give you another Advocate, to be with you forever. This is the Spirit of truth, whom the world cannot receive, because it neither sees him nor knows him. You know him, because he abides with you, and he will be in you" (John 14:16, 17).**

> **"[T]he Advocate, the Holy Spirit, whom the Father will send in my name, will teach you everything, and remind you of all that I have said to you. Peace I leave with you; my peace I give to you. I do not**

give to you as the world gives. Do not let your hearts be troubled, and do not let them be afraid" (John 14:26, 27).

"When the Advocate comes, whom I will send to you from the Father, the Spirit of truth who comes from the Father, he will testify on my behalf" (John 15:26).

"When the Spirit of truth comes, he will guide you into all the truth; for he will not speak on his own, but will speak whatever he hears, and he will declare to you the things that are to come. He will glorify me, because he will take what is mine and declare it to you. All that the Father has is mine. For this reason I said that he will take what is mine and declare it to you" (John 16:13–15).

Ask of Him

You might ask: How can the Holy Spirit Renewal become real for me?
Why not begin your journey with what our Lord said?
Consider what our Lord revealed to us:

"So I say to you, Ask, and it will be given you; search, and you will find; knock, and the door will be opened for you. For everyone who asks receives, and everyone who searches finds, and for everyone who knocks, the door will be opened. Is there anyone among you who, if your child asks for a fish, will give a snake instead of a fish? Or if the child asks for an egg, will give a scorpion? If

you then, who are evil, know how to give good gifts to your children, how much more will the heavenly Father give the Holy Spirit to those who ask him!" (Luke 11:9–13).

Ask of Him.
Open the door of your heart to Him.

Humility

Listen to what He said to us: **"I came that they may have life, and have it abundantly" (John 10:10).**
Living life in abundance is founded upon humility to the will of God.
If it is the will of our Lord for the Holy Spirit to overflow in power, then let us respond with humility.
Divine signs are designed to accompany our witness in our walk with our Lord. We can be zealous for these gifts. This is how we can line up our spiritual will with the will of the Holy Spirit: being zealous for spiritual gifts. This is our God-given right as Christians.

Our Lord's Return

Finally, at The Last Supper, Christ not only promised us the Holy Spirit, but He also promised to return for us. He also explained to us the way (the path) to the Father in Heaven: Through Him! Our Lord gave us this hope:

"'Do not let your hearts be troubled. Believe in God, believe also in me. In my Father's house there are many dwelling places. If it were not so, would I have told you that I go to prepare a place

for you? And if I go and prepare a place for you, I will come again and will take you to myself, so that where I am, there you may be also. And you know the way to the place where I am going.' Thomas said to him, 'Lord, we do not know where you are going. How can we know the way?' Jesus said to him, 'I am the way, and the truth, and the life. No one comes to the Father except through me'" (John 14:1–6).

[1] E. W. Bullinger, *A Critical Lexicon and Concordance to the English and Greek New Testament*, (Grand Rapids, MI: Zondervan Publishing House, 1995), p. 626.

5
Peter

"This Jesus God raised up, and of that all of us are witnesses. Being therefore exalted at the right hand of God, and having received from the Father the promise of the Holy Spirit, he has poured out this that you both see and hear."

—Peter (Acts 2:32, 33)

The book in the Bible known as the Book of Acts documents the apostles' acts in the first century A.D. It is not just a history book. It is our guide. It is our standard for living holy doctrine.

How do we know this?

The letters written by the apostles and the prophecies given by Christ confirm it.

In the Book of Acts, we see the following:

*Ascension Day & Christ's Prophecies
*Pentecost
*Apostles' Acts & Prophecies
*The Holy Spirit overflowing in Power
*The Birth and Expansion of the Church

Ascension Day

Now, let us look at the record of this magnificent day:

"While staying with them, he [Jesus] ordered them not to leave Jerusalem, but to wait there for the promise of the Father. **'This,' he said, 'is what you have heard from me; for John baptized with water, but you will be**

baptized with the Holy Spirit not many days from now.'… '[Y]ou will receive power when the Holy Spirit has come upon you; and you will be my witnesses in Jerusalem, in all Judea and Samaria, and to the ends of the earth.' When he had said this, as they were watching, he was lifted up, and a cloud took him out of their sight" (Acts 1:4, 5, 8, 9).

Pentecost

Pentecost is known as the "Birthday of the Church." (It is the birthday of our precious Catholic Faith.) This is because Christ poured out the Holy Spirit and, by doing so, created a brand-new kingdom on Earth: His Church.

Now, for the first time in history, worshipers of God could be born of God—born into Christ's kingdom by spiritual birth: born from above by the Holy Spirit. Thus, Christ's Church was "born." And our Lord gave His Church a new language: new tongues.

Here is the record of our Lord pouring out the Holy Spirit:

"When the day of Pentecost had come, they were all together in one place. And suddenly from heaven there came a sound like the rush of a violent wind, and it filled the entire house where they were sitting. Divided tongues, as of fire, appeared among them, and a tongue rested on each of them. All of them were filled with the Holy Spirit and began to speak in other languages, as the Spirit gave them ability" (Acts 2:1–4).

This mystifying display of supernatural power caused the worshipers at the temple to be struck with awe:

"Now there were devout Jews from every nation under heaven living in Jerusalem. And at this sound the crowd gathered and was bewildered, because each one heard them speaking in the native language of each. Amazed and astonished, they asked, 'Are not all these who are speaking Galileans? And how is it that we hear, each of us, in our own native language?'" (Acts 2:5–8).

"'[I]n our own languages we hear them speaking about God's deeds of power.' All were amazed and perplexed, saying to one another, 'What does this mean?' But others sneered and said, 'They are filled with new wine.' But Peter, standing with the eleven, raised his voice and addressed them, 'Men of Judea and all who live in Jerusalem, let this be known to you, and listen to what I say. Indeed, these are not drunk, as you suppose, for it is only nine o'clock in the morning. No, this is what was spoken through the prophet Joel':

"In the last days it will be, God declares, that I will pour out my Spirit upon all flesh, and your sons and your daughters shall prophesy, and your young men shall see visions, and your old men shall dream dreams. Even upon my slaves, both men and women, in those days I will pour out my Spirit; and they shall prophesy'"" (Acts 2:11–18).

In order to establish the significance of what the crowd witnessed, Peter quoted the prophet Joel (one of the Old Testament prophets). Peter told the crowd they had heard divine prophecy fulfilled in their ears. Joel foretold that God would pour out His Spirit—and He did.

On Pentecost, the power of the Holy Spirit overflowed into new tongues.

Yet for all of this, Isaiah (another Old Testament prophet) foretold there would be Israelites who would reject even a supernatural sign from God (new tongues). On Pentecost, some Israelites even accused Peter of being drunk when he spoke in tongues. (The joy in the Holy Spirit exhibited by the disciples was misunderstood to be drunkenness!)

Peter told the crowd that mocking the sign of the Holy Spirit language is wrong; it was God's plan all along. Peter shrugged off the accusations and took center stage as he stood up to address the crowd. Without fear, Peter began to teach the Good News of salvation in Christ. The result of Peter's great oration was the acceptance of Christ by about 3,000 souls on that very day.

Interestingly, just 50 days earlier, Peter had been hiding behind locked doors, "for fear of the Jews" (John 20:19). But now, filled with spiritual power, Peter changed. No longer controlled by fear, Peter became a man of great confidence and faith.

The Holy Spirit EXPERIENCE transformed Peter.

Peter had a new set of eyes with which to view life.

The apostle looked quite differently on those whom he once feared when he gave the crowd the Good News:

"You that are Israelites, listen to what I have to say: Jesus of Nazareth, a man attested to you by God with deeds of power, wonders, and signs that God did through him among you, as you yourselves know—this man, handed over to you according to the definite plan and foreknowledge of God, you crucified and killed by the hands of those outside the law. But God raised him up, having freed him from death, because it was impossible for him to be held in its power.... This Jesus God raised up, and of that all of us are witnesses. Being therefore exalted at the right hand of God, and having received from the Father the promise of the Holy Spirit, he has poured out this that you both see and hear" (Acts 2:22–24, 32, 33).

"'Therefore let the entire house of Israel know with certainty that God has made him both Lord and Messiah, this Jesus whom you crucified.' Now when they heard this, they were cut to the heart and said to Peter and to the other apostles, 'Brothers, what should we do?' Peter said to them, 'Repent, and be baptized every one of you in the name of Jesus Christ so that your sins may be forgiven; and you will receive the gift of the Holy Spirit. For the promise is for you, for your children, and for all who are far away, everyone whom the Lord our God calls to him.' And he testified with many other arguments and exhorted them, saying, 'Save yourselves from this corrupt generation.' So those who welcomed his message were baptized, and that day about three thousand persons were added. They devoted themselves to the apostles' teaching and fellowship, to the breaking of bread and the prayers" (Acts 2:36–42).

"Brothers, what shall we do?"
"Repent and be baptized, every one of you, in the name of Jesus Christ for the forgiveness of your sins. And you will receive the gift of the Holy Spirit."

This question and Peter's response are just as alive and real today as they were some 2,000 years ago. The promises of God are unchanging.

Imagine what could have been going through the mind of Peter. Ten days earlier, he had watched Christ ascend off the planet. Now Jerusalem was filled with the Good News, and it would soon spread to surrounding areas.

6
Luke

"On hearing this, they were baptized in the name of the Lord Jesus. When Paul had laid his hands on them, the Holy Spirit came upon them, and they spoke in tongues and prophesied."

—Luke (Acts 19:5, 6)

Luke—who wrote the Book of Acts—gave us three examples of people who spoke forth the divine sign of new tongues: Israelites, Gentiles (non-Israelites), and disciples of John the Baptist (who were baptized with water).

The Israelites

As covered in the previous chapter, the first group of people to receive the Holy Spirit Baptism and speak in the Holy Spirit language were Israelites (Christ's disciples). And, with this Holy Spirit Baptism, the disciples became the first Christians.

(The Holy Spirit is also referred to as the "Spirit of Christ" (Rom. 8:9). Thus, when we are filled with the Spirit of Christ, we have Christ within us; we are Christians.)

After Pentecost, the new Christians (the disciples) carried the Good News beyond the temple area to the Gentiles.

The Gentiles

To prepare the Gentiles (the Romans) for their Holy Spirit EXPERIENCE, Christ first sent an angel:

"In Caesarea there was a man named Cornelius, a centurion of the Italian Cohort, as it was called. He was a devout man who feared God with all his household; he gave alms generously to the people and prayed constantly to God. One afternoon at about three o'clock he had a vision in which he clearly saw an angel of God coming in and saying to him, 'Cornelius.' He stared at him in terror and said, 'What is it, Lord?' He answered, 'Your prayers and your alms have ascended as a memorial before God. Now send men to Joppa for a certain Simon who is called Peter; he is lodging with Simon, a tanner, whose house is by the seaside.' When the angel who spoke to him had left, he called two of his slaves and a devout soldier from the ranks of those who served him, and after telling them everything, he sent them to Joppa" (Acts 10:1–8).

Peter's Mission

After hearing from Cornelius' men, Peter traveled with them to the home of Cornelius. Upon arriving, Peter addressed Cornelius: "may I ask why you have sent for me?" (Acts 10:29).

"Cornelius replied, 'Four days ago at this very hour, at three o'clock, I was praying in my house when suddenly a man in dazzling clothes stood before me. He said, "Cornelius, your prayer has been heard and your alms have been remembered before God. Send therefore to Joppa and ask for Simon, who is called Peter; he is staying in the home of Simon, a tanner, by the sea." Therefore I sent for you immediately, and you have been kind enough to come. So now all of us are here in the presence of God to listen to all that the Lord has commanded you to say.'

"Then Peter began to speak to them: 'I truly understand that God shows no partiality, but in every nation anyone who fears him and does what is right is acceptable to him. You know the message he sent to the people of Israel, preaching peace by Jesus Christ—he is Lord of all. That message spread throughout Judea, beginning in Galilee after the baptism that John announced: how God anointed Jesus of Nazareth with the Holy Spirit and with power; how he went about doing good and healing all who were oppressed by the devil, for God was with him. We are witnesses to all that he did both in Judea and in Jerusalem. They put him to death by hanging him on a tree; but God raised him on the third day and allowed him to appear, not to all the people but to us who were chosen by God as witnesses, and who ate and drank with him after he rose from the dead. He commanded us to preach to the people and to testify that he is the one ordained by God as judge of the living and the dead. All the prophets testify about him that everyone who believes in him receives forgiveness of sins through his name' (Acts 10:30–43).

"While Peter was still speaking, the Holy Spirit fell upon all who heard the word. The circumcised believers who had come with Peter were astounded that the gift of the Holy Spirit had been poured out even on the Gentiles, for they heard them speaking in tongues and extolling God" (Acts 10:44–46).

After Peter taught the Good News, the Romans believed and received the Holy Spirit—and spoke in new tongues.
As Christ had prophesied, new tongues are a divine sign. This is how Peter (and those with him) knew the Romans had

been baptized: the visual and audible power the Holy Spirit (in the form of new tongues).

This is the New Covenant that Christ gave to every nation, to every bloodline: Baptism with the Holy Spirit, and gifts of the Holy Spirit.

Disciples of John the Baptist

When Paul visited the city of Ephesus, he taught 12 disciples about Christ's Baptism, and they spoke in new tongues:

> "Paul passed through the interior regions and came to Ephesus, where he found some disciples. He said to them, 'Did you receive the Holy Spirit when you became believers?' They replied, 'No, we have not even heard that there is a Holy Spirit.' Then he said, 'Into what then were you baptized?' They answered, 'Into John's baptism.'

> "Paul said, 'John baptized with the baptism of repentance, telling the people to believe in the one who was to come after him, that is, in Jesus.' On hearing this, they were baptized in the name of the Lord Jesus. When Paul had laid his hands on them, the Holy Spirit came upon them, and they spoke in tongues and prophesied—altogether there were about twelve of them" (Acts 19:1–7).

Paul asked a good question: "Did you receive the Holy Spirit when you became believers?" This question is just as valid today as it was in the first century A.D. Paul explained to these disciples exactly what John the Baptist prophesied:

> "I baptize you with water for repentance, but one who is more powerful than I is coming after me; I am not worthy

to carry his sandals. He will baptize you with the Holy Spirit and fire" (Matt. 3:11).

First Century Testimony

On Pentecost, our Lord baptized His disciples with the Holy Spirit—and they spoke in new tongues.

Our Lord baptized Cornelius and his company with the Holy Spirit—and they spoke in new tongues.

Our Lord baptized the Ephesians with the Holy Spirit—and they spoke in new tongues.

It all goes back to John the Baptist: He prophesied of the Holy Spirit Baptism with fire!

"That 'fire' Baptism gave me the 'fire' of God's love!"
—Father Ray

7
Paul

"For it is the God who said, 'Let light shine out of darkness,' who has shone in our hearts to give the light of the knowledge of the glory of God in the face of Jesus Christ. But we have this treasure in clay jars, so that it may be made clear that this extraordinary power belongs to God and does not come from us."

—Paul (2 Cor. 4:6, 7)

We, as God's creation, are clay jars (earthen vessels). And in our earthen vessels, God placed His treasure: "the light of the knowledge of the glory of God in the face of Jesus Christ" and "extraordinary power."

This divine light is the Gospel of the Good News.

God testified (and continues to testify) to the Good News of salvation by extraordinary power: signs, wonders, and miracles.

Now, let us read another record: God testifying to our salvation.

"It [salvation] was declared at first through the Lord, and it was attested to us by those who heard him, while God added his testimony by signs and wonders and various miracles, and by gifts of the Holy Spirit, distributed according to his will" (Heb. 2:3, 4).

Thankfully, there is no need to wonder about God testifying in your life through the gift of new tongues. If you are filled with the Holy Spirit, then the Holy Spirit can overflow with power. And God can testify in your life; you can speak the language that Christ gave us: the Holy Spirit language of His Church.

> Christ gave this charismatic sign to His apostles.
> Christ gave us examples in the Book of Acts.
> Christ showed us the will of the Holy Spirit.

Christ revealed to Paul the will of the Holy Spirit: "I would like all of you to speak in tongues" (1 Cor. 14:5). And then Paul gave us insight into his own spiritual life: "I thank God that I speak in tongues more than all of you" (1 Cor. 14:18). In essence, Paul told us the importance of the Holy Spirit language. He chose to follow the will of the Holy Spirit.

> We in Christ's Church can embrace the will of the Holy Spirit.
> And why not?
> The gift of new tongues is direct, perfect, spiritual worship of God.
> And with our divine language, we can pray perfectly unto God.
> And with our divine language, we can sing perfectly unto God.
> And with our divine language, we can speak perfectly unto God.

Paul said:

"For those who speak in a tongue do not speak to other people but to God; for nobody understands them, since they are speaking mysteries in the Spirit.... What should I do then? I will pray with the spirit, but I will pray with the mind also; I will sing praise with the spirit, but I will sing praise with the mind also" (1 Cor. 14:2, 15).

And Paul said: "Be imitators of me, as I am of Christ" (1 Cor. 11:1).
Let us imitate Paul.
Let us long for the Holy Spirit EXPERIENCE.
Let us speak, sing, and pray in the Holy Spirit language—just as Paul did.
Allow yourself to KNOW what it really means to be made NEW:

"For the love of Christ urges us on, because we are convinced that one has died for all; therefore all have died. And he died for all, so that those who live might live no longer for themselves, but for him who died and was raised for them. From now on, therefore, we regard no one from a human point of view; even though we once knew Christ from a human point of view, we know him no longer in that way. So if anyone is in Christ, there is a new creation: everything old has passed away; see, everything has become new!" (2 Cor. 5:14–17).

Our Generation

In the first century A.D., the disciples were revolutionary. Never in recorded history had man spoken forth a language inspired by the Holy Spirit. In the twenty-first century, it is still revolutionary to speak forth a language inspired by the Holy Spirit.
And you can be revolutionary too! It is your choice.

Christ our King gave this divine sign to His Church in the first century, and it remains just as valid in the twenty-first century.

Paul told us all gifts of the Spirit will remain within the Church until the Second Advent: when the glorified Christ is revealed to the world and returns for us. Paul's prophecy is unmistakable:

> "[I]n every way you have been enriched in him, in speech and knowledge of every kind—just as the testimony of Christ has been strengthened among you—so that you are not lacking in any spiritual gift as you wait for the revealing of our Lord Jesus Christ. He will also strengthen you to the end, so that you may be blameless on the day of our Lord Jesus Christ" (1 Cor. 1:5–8).

Paul handed us Christ's revelation.

If Paul said, "you are not lacking in any spiritual gift as you wait for the revealing of our Lord Jesus Christ" then logically, until our Lord Jesus Christ is revealed, His kingdom cannot lack any spiritual gift. Thereby, God continues to demonstrate the extraordinary power by all gifts of the Holy Spirit, including the gift of "various kinds of tongues" (1 Cor. 12:10).

This EXPERIENCE is powerful—yet at the same time, gentle and peaceful.

Here is what Paul told us about the Holy Spirit:

> "[T]he fruit of the Spirit is love, joy, peace, patience, kindness, generosity, faithfulness, gentleness, and self-control.... If we live by the Spirit, let us also be guided by the Spirit" (Gal. 5:22, 23, 25).

Everything the Son of God and the apostle Paul heralded about the Good News is still the Good News! Thank God!

8
James

"God opposes the proud, but gives grace to the humble."

—James (4:6)

James wrote to us about the power of the "tongue" to bless... or curse. Let us heed the message of James:

> "[L]ook at ships: though they are so large that it takes strong winds to drive them, yet they are guided by a very small rudder wherever the will of the pilot directs. So also the tongue is a small member, yet it boasts of great exploits. How great a forest is set ablaze by a small fire! And the tongue is a fire. The tongue is placed among our members as a world of iniquity; it stains the whole body, sets on fire the cycle of nature, and is itself set on fire by hell. For every species of beast and bird, of reptile and sea creature, can be tamed and has been tamed by the human species, but no one can tame the tongue—a restless evil, full of deadly poison. With it we bless the Lord and Father, and with it we curse those who are made in the likeness of God. From the same mouth come blessing and cursing. My brothers and sisters, this ought not to be so. Does a spring pour forth from the same opening both fresh and brackish water? Can a fig tree, my brothers and sisters, yield olives, or a grapevine figs? No more can salt water yield fresh" (James 3:4–12).

And James revealed to us that when we humble ourselves before our God, He lifts us up:

"[W]hoever wishes to be a friend of the world becomes an enemy of God. Or do you suppose that it is for nothing that the scripture says, 'God yearns jealously for the spirit that he has made to dwell in us'? But he gives all the more grace; therefore it says, 'God opposes the proud, but gives grace to the humble.' Submit yourselves therefore to God. Resist the devil, and he will flee from you. Draw near to God, and he will draw near to you.... Humble yourselves before the Lord, and he will exalt you" (James 4:4–8, 10).

9
Jude

"But you, beloved, build yourselves up on your most holy faith; pray in the Holy Spirit."

—Jude (20)

Jude exhorted us and warned us. He is speaking to all generations of Christians. We do well to take heed.

Exhortation

"Beloved, while eagerly preparing to write to you about the salvation we share, I find it necessary to write and appeal to you to contend for the faith that was once for all entrusted to the saints" (Jude 3).

Warning

Jude is then compelled to warn fellow believers of immoral men circulating in the Church. These "intruders" appeared to profess the faith—yet brought evil into Church.

"For certain intruders have stolen in among you, people who long ago were designated for this condemnation as ungodly, who pervert the grace of our God into licentiousness [immoderation] and deny our only Master and Lord, Jesus Christ.... [T]hese people slander whatever they do not understand" (Jude 4, 10).

Exhortation

Jude concludes by speaking to those who contend for the faith:

"But you, beloved, build yourselves up on your most holy faith; pray in the Holy Spirit; keep yourselves in the love of God; look forward to the mercy of our Lord Jesus Christ that leads to eternal life.... Now to him who is able to keep you from falling, and to make you stand without blemish in the presence of his glory with rejoicing, to the only God our Savior, through Jesus Christ our Lord, be glory, majesty, power, and authority, before all time and now and forever. Amen" (Jude 20, 21, 24, 25).

Let us contend for the Faith.
Let us hear the voice of our Holy Fathers.
Let us hear the voice of Charismatic Catholics.
Let us embrace the Catholic Charismatic Renewal.
Let us pray, speak, and sing in the Holy Spirit language.
Let us heed the work of Christ and the Holy Spirit in our Church.
Let us hear the voices of Christ, Peter, Luke, Paul, James, and Jude.

May God bless
YOUR HOLY SPIRIT RENEWAL EXPERIENCE!

AMEN!!

Addenda

Addenda available online at En Route Books and Media (see https://enroutebooksandmedia.com/charismaticrenewal/) will give you additional insight and resources regarding the ongoing work of Catholic Charismatic Renewal.

Acknowledgments

First let me say I am grateful for Dr. William Ayles. He initiated the development of this book and worked with me to bring it into fruition.

—Father Ray Introvigne

Together, we would like to thank our editor, The Persnickety Proofreader, who did a marvelous job getting this ready for production.

Finally, we are eternally grateful for the Father, the Son, and the Holy Spirit. Our Lord Jesus Christ saved us, baptized us, and granted us His precious gift of the Holy Spirit language. We thank God for the Catholic Charismatic Renewal.

www.ingramcontent.com/pod-product-compliance
Lightning Source LLC
LaVergne TN
LVHW051844080426
835512LV00018B/3064